Fresh Canadian
Bistro

Top Canadian chefs
share their favourite recipes

Craig Flinn

Formac Publishing Company Limited

For Mum, with love

Photo Credits

All interior photos by Alanna Jankov, except where noted below:

Craig Flinn (sketches): 10-11, 30-31, 48-49, 86-87, 106-107, 132-133; iStock: 2, 3, 8 (background), 9-10,15, 27, 30-31, 48-49, 75, 79, 86-87, 97, 106-107, 111, 115, 119, 120, 121, 127, 128, 132-133, 152, 156; 88; Restaurant Les Fougères: 69, 137; River Café: 13; Rouge: 19

Formac Publishing Company Limited recognizes the support of the Province of Nova Scotia through the Department of Tourism, Culture and Heritage. We acknowledge the financial support of the Government of Canada through the Book Publishing Industry Development Program (BPIDP) for our publishing activities.

NOVA SCOTIA
Tourism, Culture and Heritage

National Library of Canada Cataloguing in Publication

Flinn, Craig
    Fresh Canadian Bistro: top Canadian chefs share their favourite recipes/ Craig Flinn.

ISBN 978-0-88780-853-1

    1. Cookery, Canadian. I. Title.

TX715.6.F56 2009   641.5'64   C2009-902276-1

Formac Publishing Company Limited
5502 Atlantic Street
Halifax, Nova Scotia
B3H 1G4
www.formac.ca

Printed and bound in China

Contents

Seasons

Within each chapter, the recipes are categorized by season to help you make the most out of fresh and locally produced fruits, vegetables, meats, fish and artisan food products. The following graphics highlight when the recipe ingredients are freshest and most readily available from local sources. As an additional reference, the Seasonal Recipe Index (pg. 158) will let you shift your cooking selections with the seasons.

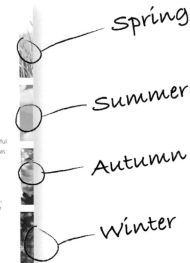

Spring

Summer

Autumn

Winter

Panisse with Roasted Teardrop Tomatoes and Olive Tapenade

Renee Lavallée, Five Fishermen, Halifax, Nova Scotia

Panisse is a simple chickpea-flour bread that is fried until crispy. The dish originates from the area around Nice in France. Renee has paired it with wonderful little tomatoes that you can find from greenhouse growers year-round. Roasting brings out the sweetness that is sometimes lacking in off-season tomatoes. This is a summery dish that can be enjoyed during colder weather as a vegetarian appetizer or with a piece of roasted fish like halibut or cod.

Panisse
3 cups (750 mL) water
¼ cup (60 mL) extra-virgin olive oil
2 tsp (10 mL) salt
1 ½ cups (375 mL) chickpea flour
2 tbsp (30 mL) finely sliced (chiffonade) fresh basil
¼ tsp (1 mL) freshly ground black pepper
¼ cup (60 mL) olive oil (for pan frying)

Roasted Teardrop Tomatoes
2 cups (500 mL) red and yellow teardrop tomatoes
3 tbsp (45 mL) extra-virgin olive oil
several sprigs thyme
2 cloves garlic, peeled and sliced
¼ tsp (1 mL) salt
¼ tsp (1 mL) pepper

Tapenade
1 cup (250 mL) pitted Kalamata olives
1 anchovy fillet
1 clove garlic
zest of 1 lemon
¼ to ⅓ cup (60 to 85 mL) extra-virgin olive oil
salt and pepper to taste

For the panisse:
Bring water, oil and salt to a low boil. Whisk in chickpea flour, being careful to prevent lumps. Stir with a wooden spoon, about 10 minutes, until it has a thick consistency, similar to porridge. Add basil and adjust seasonings.

Pour panisse mixture onto a greased baking sheet to a thickness of about ½ in (1 cm) and refrigerate for 2 hours. Cut into desired shapes, such as circles, triangles or rectangular strips. Preheat a nonstick or well-seasoned cast iron pan on high, add olive oil and fry anisse on both sides, until golden brown. Thicker panisse portions may need to bake for 5 or 7 minutes in a 350°F (180°C) oven to finish cooking.

Place a hot piece of panisse in the centre of each plate and top with a liberal amount of tapenade (about 2 tbsp/30 mL or so). Add 3 or 4 tomatoes on top and garnish with a few leaves of thyme if desired.

Serves 8, with leftovers

For the roasted tomatoes:
Preheat oven to 400°F (200°C) and place tomatoes on a baking tray. Drizzle generously with olive oil, thyme sprigs, garlic, salt and pepper. Mix everything together with your hands (they're your best tool for this job) and roast for 10 to 15 minutes, or until the tomatoes are splitting on their sides. Remove from oven and set aside, but make sure to keep cooled tomatoes in their roasting liquids.

For the tapenade: In a food processor, mix olives, anchovy, garlic and lemon zest together with a little olive oil. Start to purée while adding a slow stream of olive oil. This should be a fairly loose tapenade, so don't worry about adding too much oil. Check for seasonings, and set aside.

Yields 1 ½ cups (325 mL)

Hot & Cold Appetizers 81

Acknowledgements

This book would not have been possible without the help of many, many people.

To the chefs who contributed their ideas and time, I thank you. Chefs and cooks do not work from nine to five and usually do these extra projects on their own time, taking even more time away from their families. I appreciate this effort more than words can express.

A special thank you to the staff at Chives, who covered for me on many nights as I wrote instead of cooking at their side on the line. A special thank you to Darren Lewis, George Davis, Betty Bartel and Brady Muller for running the day-to-day operations of the restaurant and café, for taking care of our guests and for supporting my crazy ideas.

Thank you to the recipe team who tested and helped with the food styling: Bob and Janine Durning, John Corney, Eber Serieys, Jonathan James and Natasha Jollymore.

Lots of love and appreciation to the design and editing team at Formac who have the creativity to make ideas and words on paper look so wonderful. Thank you Alanna for your eye and your help in producing such great photographs. You have made the recipes come to life.

Thanks Greg for all the words of wisdom and unconditional support in cooking — and life.

As always we cooks would have nothing to work with if it weren't for the food producers and growers of our great nation. You make us look good when it is you who deserve the applause.

And finally a special thank you to my family, especially Jason, Caroline and Jack, for providing inspiration at the end of the hardest days.

– C. F.

Foreword

I first met Craig Flinn in 2004 during the Gold Medal Plates culinary championships in Halifax, Nova Scotia. Two years later we again found ourselves together in Piedmont, Italy attending the Terra Madre conference, a huge multinational meeting of food producers, food educators and chefs who live by the principles of the Slow Food movement in their support of locally sourced foods produced in an environmentally responsible way. Craig's dedication to this type of cooking and his passion for understanding Canadian food has always been evident to me.

In September 2008 I organized an event at Eigensinn Farm, my home near Collingwood, Ontario. I had the idea of assembling chefs and cooks from across Canada for a meeting of minds and menus. The first Canadian Chefs' Congress was the result. Chefs were chosen from each province and territory to prepare regional dishes for the nearly 500 attendees. Craig's dedication and passion for Canadian food and local, sustainable food sourcing made him the natural choice to represent Nova Scotia.

My aim with the congress was to nurture a network of young cooks who, though spread out over huge distances, would stand united in support of a better type of cooking — a sustainable, responsible and culturally strong representation of Canadian food. During the congress Craig spoke of his desire to write a book that attempted to continue that trend. His concept was to unite chefs through a collection of recipes — recipes that would paint a portrait of Canadian food today, as seen through the eyes of some of the country's best working cooks.

Many of the chefs whose recipes are featured in this book have visited my farm and have cooked by my side. We all share the same desire to cook using the very best local, seasonal and environmentally sustainable ingredients we can find. It is this love, perhaps more than our love of cooking, that unites us all as Canadian chefs and may, one day, lead us to a better understanding of our Canadian cuisine.

– Michael Stadtlander

What is Bistro?

Many great culinary adventures have occurred as a result of my little restaurant, Chives Canadian Bistro, which opened on Barrington Street in Halifax in 2001. Since then I have also had the privilege of cooking, eating and travelling with the best of the best in this country. With every recipe tested, every dinner served and every plate washed and put away, always for me there were questions. What is Canadian cooking? Is the definition important or even possible in a land so young and so diverse? And what on earth is a Canadian bistro?

There is a strong desire among the chefs in this great country to cook with locally sourced and seasonally inspired ingredients. Except for using the odd lemon, vanilla bean or cinnamon stick, young Canadian chefs are passionate promoters of their local farmers, fishermen, artisan cheese and charcuterie producers and wine makers. Their menus are generally small, they avoid convenience products like powdered hollandaise and little frozen dinner rolls, and they change as frequently as the weather. My mentor, Chef Michael Smith, once said to me during a prep session, "What is more 'Canadian' than a Canadian cook using Canadian-grown ingredients in Canada?"

But something else became evident to me in the fall of 2004 as I travelled across Canada, staging (volunteer cooking) at some of the best restaurants in the country. Even the most modern and high-end dining rooms were serving dishes that could be traced back to the bistros, trattorias, stubes and pubs I used to frequent when I was an apprentice chef in Europe. Braised meats, ragouts, handmade pastas and gnocchi, or a simple piece of just-caught fish topped with browned butter, a hunk of delicious stinky cheese and a perfect loaf of bread — these ethnic, Old-World peasant dishes had become the stars of our new Canadian cooking. The only difference was where and how the ingredients were sourced.

Humankind has a long history of trading and borrowing cultural characteristics. We borrow ideas from food-loving nations. We think of pasta as being Italian, yet noodles were first eaten by the Chinese two thousand years ago. The Swiss and Belgians get all the credit for being the world's chocolatiers when the sweet treat actually came from Mexico and Central America. In the modern world, where air travel is so easy and high-speed Internet is so accessible, ideas change hands faster than ever before. It has become the norm for apprenticing cooks to travel the world to gain experience, and these cooks bring new ideas to their menus. The result is a culture where palates are complex and generalities about our food difficult to state. The best we can do is look at smaller areas within our country, provinces and cities, and look at the food we find to be regional — but no less Canadian than any other region.

This book does not attempt to define Canadian bistro cooking in words. The collection of recipes is the definition. These recipes provide a snapshot of the dishes that chefs are cooking right now across this vast land. The restaurants featured here do not all call themselves either Canadian or bistros specifically, but they surely are representative of the style of cooking that I fell in love with many years ago. This is what fresh Canadian bistro cooking is to the leading chefs of our time.

Read these recipes, cook them, taste them and share them. This is the food we are all enjoying in the bistros and restaurants of Canada.

Soups, Chowders & Ragouts

For most Canadians soup is comfort food, although there is a long and complex history to soup-making. Classically trained chefs learn about the importance of a simple stock and how to transform it into an elegant consommé. They learn how an egg yolk and a splash of cream whisked together (called a liaison) brings silky richness to a vegetable purée. They spend days and weeks in culinary schools learning about ragouts, stews, blanquettes, potages, fricassees and so on.

In reality these dishes were originally created to avoid wasting food when families had very little. Whether the carcass of a turkey was simmered after Thanksgiving or the last few beets in the root cellar were boiled and puréed into borscht, leftovers usually found their way into the soup pot. In nearly every bistro in Canada or Europe, there is always a soup du jour simmering, and my guess is that the chef is trying to use up the last of something in the fridge. But creative chefs like to take this one step further and add flair to the simple soup. In modern restaurants soup is more than chicken noodle or beef and barley. It is an opportunity to show off one dominant flavour, or perhaps two, in an elegant forum. Garnishes are added to complement the theme ingredient or ingredients, and a perfect balance is the ultimate goal.

Chowder, that East Coast delicacy, could more accurately be called "fisherman's soup" and be described as a milk-and-potato-thickened broth using whatever fish was landed that day. Stews and ragouts are ways to simmer and tenderize tougher cuts of meat. Less "brothy" than soups, they often make up the main course of a meal and are served with a starch like potatoes, noodles, dumplings or good bread. The term ragout has also widened in meaning to include vegetables, not just meat, and now ragouts featuring mushrooms, root vegetables and tomatoes are common bistro choices.

In this chapter you will find recipes that touch on most of these themes. As always the recipes feature seasonal ingredients, and I encourage you to use whatever you have to produce your very own soup du jour.

Asparagus, Fiddlehead and White Bean Soup

Scott Pohorelic, River Café, Calgary, Alberta

If you were to name two vegetables that sing of springtime in Canada they would certainly be asparagus and fiddleheads. Both are essentially very young wild perennials, though of course we now have cultivated asparagus even during the high season in late spring. Fiddleheads are still almost exclusively hand foraged but are eagerly anticipated each year by diehard vegetable lovers for their grassy, aromatic flavour. Scott Pohorelic has created a cuisine in Calgary that represents not only Western cooking but touches on nearly every province in the country. This light and refreshing spring soup could be found on a bistro menu in New Brunswick as well as Alberta.

1 tsp (5 mL) minced ginger root

1 tsp (5 mL) minced garlic

1 tbsp (15 mL) minced shallot

1 bulb fennel, minced

1 tsp (5 mL) cooking oil

¼ cup (60 mL) dry white wine

½ tsp (3 mL) whole black peppercorns

1 bay leaf

4 juniper berries

½ yellow onion, chopped

½ carrot, chopped

8 cups (2 L) cold water

1 tsp (5 mL) chopped fresh thyme

1 tsp (5 mL) chopped fresh oregano

1 tsp (5 mL) fresh lemon juice

1 tsp (5 mL) grainy mustard

2 cups (500 mL) cooked white beans

1 lb (450 g) beech mushrooms

1 tbsp (15 mL) vegetable oil

1 cup (250 mL) fresh asparagus, blanched and cut into 1-in (3-cm) pieces

1 cup (250 mL) fresh fiddleheads, rinsed, blanched and rinsed again

In a pot, sauté ginger, garlic, shallot and fennel in cooking oil over medium heat for 10 minutes, or until tender. Be careful not to let mixture brown. Add white wine to deglaze pot.

Place peppercorns, bay leaf, juniper berries, onion and carrot in a piece of cheesecloth and tie it up to make a sachet (spice bag). Add water, thyme, oregano, lemon juice, mustard, cooked beans and sachet to the pot. Bring to a low simmer.

In a hot frying pan, sauté mushrooms in oil quickly and add to the pot. Season generously with salt and continue to simmer for 20 minutes. Just before serving, add asparagus and fiddleheads and adjust seasoning once more.

Serves 8 to 10

Sea Urchin and Jerusalem Artichoke Soup with Hazelnut Oil

Robert Clark, C Restaurant, Vancouver, British Columbia

Robert Clark is the type of chef all of us should aspire to be: talented, knowledgeable and responsible. No cook in our country has taken a more prominent stance towards sustainable seafood practices than Robert. His food is not only delicious and creative, it challenges us to think about what we are eating. The delicious Jerusalem artichoke soup he offers here is creamy, with an earthiness similar to wild mushrooms. The addition of sea urchin to the purée adds a heightened level of flavour and richness. Robert suggests garnishing this soup with a lobe of fresh sea urchin, along with some freshly snipped chives. You can find sea urchin at top fish markets, but if you simply cannot obtain any, the Jerusalem artichoke soup is delicious on its own.

1 medium onion, coarsely chopped

1 stalk leek, white part only, cleaned and chopped

10 whole garlic cloves

2 bay leaves

3 tbsp (45 mL) unsalted butter

1 lb (450 g) peeled Jerusalem artichokes, coarsely chopped

4 cups (1 L) vegetable stock, fish stock or water

1 cup (250 mL) dry white wine

⅔ lb (300 g) fresh sea urchin

⅓ lb (150 g) unsalted butter

2 tbsp (30 mL) chives, freshly snipped

1 tsp (5 mL) high-quality hazelnut oil

Sweat onion, leek, garlic and bay leaves with butter for 5 minutes, or until translucent (no colour). Add chopped Jerusalem artichokes and cook for 3 minutes. Add stock and white wine, season and slowly simmer until artichokes are tender. Remove bay leaves and purée soup in a blender until very smooth. Strain through a sieve or fine-meshed chinois. Reserve this soup base until you are ready to serve.

Allowing 6 oz (170 g) of soup base per person, bring liquid to a boil and simmer for 1 minute. Pour into a blender and, on low to medium speed, incorporate sea urchin and butter.

Adjust seasoning and serve immediately. The soup cannot be boiled again after this step. Garnish with a whole piece of urchin, chives and a drizzle of nut oil.

Serves 6 to 8

Grosse Soupe du Petit Jardin (Hearty Garden Patch Soup)

Darren Lewis, Chives Canadian Bistro, Halifax, Nova Scotia

This summer soup really does need to be made in that relatively small window of time when your garden is in full swing, or at least when the market is teeming with beautiful tender vegetables. This is an Acadian soup that draws on Chef Darren's personal experiences growing up in New Brunswick. Acadian cooking and bistro cooking share a similar ideology in that every dish is created out of necessity and availability. "This recipe," says Darren, "was always a family summertime favourite and truly lives up to its name. If you translate it word for word it means 'big soup from the little garden.'"

3 tbsp (45 mL) reserved bacon fat, pan drippings or butter
2 yellow cooking onions, finely chopped
1 shallot, minced
2 cloves garlic, minced
2 stalks celery, finely chopped
2 cups (500 mL) baby carrots, cut in half
2 parsnips, diced
1 cup (250 mL) diced turnip
2 cups (500 mL) shredded green cabbage (not purple)
1 tbsp (15 mL) salted herbs (cured chives and parsley)
1 cup (250 mL) string beans (cut in ½-in/1-cm sections)
1 cup (250 mL) sweet peas, freshly shucked
1 cup (250 ml) kernel corn, off the cob (about 3 or 4 ears)
8 cups (2 L) homemade oxtail or beef shank broth
2 cups (500 mL) chopped garden greens (beet tops, chard or spinach)
salt and freshly ground black pepper

Heat a large stockpot on medium-high heat and add fat, onions, shallot, garlic, celery, carrots, parsnips, turnip and cabbage. Sauté until onions and cabbage are translucent. Add salted herbs, beans, peas, corn and beef broth. Bring soup to a boil and simmer for 1 hour. Add chopped greens and bring back to a boil long enough to cook greens. Adjust seasonings with salt and pepper (or some Tabasco hot sauce) and serve with good crusty bread and butter.

Yields 16 to 18 cups (8 to 9 L)

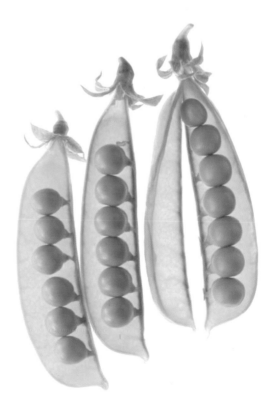

Lobster Chowder

Fish or seafood chowder is a dish that inspires visitors and residents in Canadian coastal communities to pop into a quaint bistro for lunch. A lobster chowder seems so luxurious — truly a special treat. In classic French cooking a lobster bisque is made from the shells with vegetables and a small amount of tomato. The result is a rich and creamy soup that tastes more like lobster than the meat itself. For my lobster chowder I make a simple bisque-type broth, then add potatoes and cooked lobster meat. Lobster is available year-round in Eastern Canada, but for me it remains a spring ingredient as the fishery thrives in Nova Scotia and P.E.I. at this time of year. Serve this as a lunch with freshly baked East Coast biscuits and butter.

2 cooked lobsters, meat removed, chopped and reserved
1 large onion, coarsely chopped
1 stalk celery, coarsely chopped
1 carrot, coarsely chopped
2 cloves garlic, sliced
1 bay leaf
2 sprigs fresh thyme
2 tbsp (30 mL) butter
2 tbsp (30 mL) tomato paste
2 tbsp (30 mL) flour
½ cup (125 mL) dry vermouth
4 cups (1 L) chicken broth
2 cups (500 mL) water
2 large yellow-fleshed potatoes
1 stalk leek, white part only, cleaned and chopped
1 cup (250 mL) 35% cream
salt and freshly ground pepper
fresh tarragon or chives, for garnish

Clean lobster shells under cool running water and remove head and liver. Place shells in a stockpot with onion, celery, carrot, garlic, bay leaf, thyme and butter and sauté for 10 minutes. Add tomato paste and cook for another 5 minutes. Deglaze with vermouth (or white wine) and add chicken broth. Bring to a boil and simmer for 1 hour. Top up with water when necessary.

Purée shells and vegetables and pass through a sieve or fine-meshed chinois. Add potatoes and leek and simmer until potatoes are tender, about 20 minutes. Add cream and chopped lobster meat and adjust seasonings with salt and pepper. Garnish with fresh tarragon leaves or chopped chives.

Serves 6

Watercress and Summer Leek Soup with Seared Salmon, Crème Fraîche and Caviar

I love cooking with summer leeks. They have less of the stiff green top and more of the tender white bottoms than their winter cousins. Their flavours are more subtle than other members of the onion family and they do not have an adverse effect on your breath. This soup is very simple and quick to make and can be made vegetarian by omitting the fish garnish. Farm-raised salmon has been "red-listed" for quite some time now, but efforts are being made to clean up certain aspects of the aquaculture industry. Wild salmon is the obvious choice if you are concerned about sustainability, or you can substitute char, sea trout or even a white-fleshed fish like halibut or sturgeon. The possibilities are endless. The "caviar" or salmon roe is found or attainable at most good fish markets.

Soup

1 small onion, diced

1 large summer leek (about 16 in/40 cm long), sliced and washed

1 clove garlic, sliced

3 tbsp (45 mL) butter

3 fresh thyme sprigs

¼ cup (60 mL) white wine

2 small white potatoes, diced

4 cups (1 L) vegetable or chicken stock

2 cups (500 mL) watercress, washed and stems removed

¼ cup (60 mL) 35% cream (optional)

salt and pepper to taste

Seared Salmon

12 oz (340 g) fresh boneless salmon fillet, skin-on

2 tbsp (30 mL) canola oil

salt and pepper to taste

⅓ cup (85 mL) crème fraîche

1 x 2-oz (60-g) jar salmon roe or caviar

1 tbsp (15 mL) chopped chives

For the soup:

Sauté onion, leek and garlic in butter for 3 minutes. Do not allow any colour to form. Add thyme sprigs and white wine and reduce until wine evaporates. Add potatoes and stock and bring to a boil. Cook until potatoes are tender, add watercress and bring just to a simmer. Add cream at this point, if desired. Purée in a blender while still warm, season with salt and pepper, and serve immediately.

For the salmon:

Scrape scales from salmon skin with a knife or fish-scaling tool. Cut fillet into 6 equal-sized pieces. Pinching each piece between your fingers, make two small slices in salmon skin, no more than ⅛-in (3-mm) deep. This will prevent fish from curling in the pan. Heat oil in a nonstick or cast iron frying pan. Add fish, skin side down, and cook for 4 minutes, until skin is crispy and slightly browned. Remove pan from heat and flip fish, allowing the residual heat in the pan to finish the cooking.

Presentation:

Ladle 6 to 8 oz (170 to 225 mL) of broth into a soup plate and place seared salmon in the centre of the bowl, crispy side up. Spoon a small amount of crème fraîche and a teaspoon of caviar on skin, and garnish with sliced chives or a sprig of fresh watercress.

Serves 6

French-pressed Chicken and Herb Broth with Fresh Black Summer Truffles

Paul Rogalski, Rouge, Calgary, Alberta

Truffles are typically thought of as an Italian or French ingredient, but chefs all over the world use them. In British Columbia there is a small, blossoming "trufficulture" industry that may (or may not) yield truffles in Canada, but Oregon varieties are close to home and available on the West coast. At a pinch, truffle oil can be used as a garnish for this soup. One of the most traditional French bistro soups is a clear and refreshing consommé. This is an easier and unique way to present a broth-based soup with flair. As Chef Paul writes, "I believe one of the most important things to creating great food is starting with great stocks. For this reason I like to showcase a basic chicken stock in this forward-thinking twist on a French coffee press."

Paul's Chicken Stock

4 lb (2 kg) chicken carcasses (chopped into small pieces)
1 large white onion, coarsely chopped
4 carrots, coarsely chopped
4 celery stalks, coarsely chopped
1 leek (white part only, cut in half lengthwise and washed)
2 bay leaves (fresh or dried)
2 tbsp (30 mL) sea salt
2 tbsp (30 mL) thyme leaves (dried)
2 tbsp (30 mL) whole black peppercorns
8 quarts (8 L) cold water

Broth

2 garlic cloves, slivered
2 sprigs fresh thyme
1 sprig fresh rosemary
5 crowns fresh basil
1 sprig fresh dill
2 crowns fresh lemon verbena
4 cups (1 L) simmering Paul's Chicken Stock, seasoned to
  taste (recipe above)
2 tbsp (30 mL) chopped chives
8 slices fresh black summer truffle

For Paul's chicken stock:

Roast chicken bones in a 400°F (200°C) oven for 30 minutes, or until lightly browned. In a 12-quart (12-L) stockpot, place vegetables, herbs, salt, pepper and then chicken bones. Add cold water. Cook on high heat until bubbles break through the surface, then reduce heat to low and a very soft simmer. Skim scum from surface every 10 to 15 minutes until scum subsides. Simmer uncovered for 3 to 4 hours, topping up with hot water if needed.

Carefully strain stock into another large stockpot (or heatproof container) through a fine strainer. Cool by immersing into an ice bath (a sink filled with ice and cold water). Cool to 40°F (4°C). Refrigerate overnight. Before using, carefully remove fat from surface with a slotted spoon. Freeze leftovers in small batches for further use.

Yields 24 cups (6 L)

For the broth:

Place garlic, thyme, rosemary, basil, dill and lemon verbena in a French press and carefully pour in simmering stock. Let steep for 3 minutes. In serving bowls or clear glass mugs divide chives and truffle equally. Press herbs to bottom of broth and pour over truffle and chives. Serve immediately to enjoy maximum fragrance.

Serves 4

French Pumpkin Soup

French Onion is probably the most famous bistro soup. On my parent's 40th wedding anniversary I wanted to make a simple roasted pumpkin soup for dinner. But as the day progressed, so did the soup. Before long I was hollowing out small gourds, toasting rye croutons and frying onions, and this Canadian version of a French bistro classic was born. I recommend using a strong-flavoured cheese like Quebec Oka or Gruyère in this recipe, but even a mixture of cheddar and mozzarella would be fine. However, it is essential to use small pie pumpkins and not the large "jack-o-lantern" variety to achieve the correct flavour.

Soup Base

8 cups (2 L) peeled and roughly chopped pumpkin squash
2 cups (500 mL) roughly chopped onion
1 cup (250 mL) roughly chopped celery
4 cloves garlic
½ cup (125 mL) extra-virgin olive oil
8 cups (2 L) low-sodium chicken or vegetable stock
1 tbsp (15 mL) salt
1 tbsp (15 mL) pepper
1 tsp (5 mL) grated nutmeg
¼ tsp (1 mL) ground cloves
1 cup (250 mL) 35% cream (optional)

Soup Assembly

2 medium onions, sliced
2 tbsp (30 mL) extra-virgin olive oil
¼ tsp (1 mL) salt
a few grindings of black pepper
4 slices rye bread, cubed
6 baby pumpkin squash or gourds
1 cup (250 mL) grated Oka or Gruyère cheese
2 tbsp (30 mL) toasted pumpkin seeds

For the soup base:

Preheat oven to 400°F (200°C). In a large mixing bowl, toss pumpkin, onion, celery and garlic in olive oil. Roast until pumpkin and onion begin to caramelize or turn golden brown (about 20 minutes). Place vegetables in a large stockpot and cover with stock; add salt, pepper, nutmeg and clove. Simmer for 1 hour. Purée soup carefully in a well-vented blender. Strain through a fine-meshed chinois and add cream just prior to serving.

To assemble the soup:

Preheat oven to 425°F (220°C) using the upper element (broiler). Season sliced onions with salt and pepper and sauté in olive oil until golden brown (about 15 minutes on medium heat). Place rye bread cubes on a cookie sheet and toast in the oven, stirring them every minute or two. Remove and mix them with onions.

Using a paring knife, cut tops out of baby pumpkins, as you would if making a Halloween jack-o-lantern. Scoop out seeds and pulp (the seeds can be toasted and used as garnish, or you can purchase pumpkin seeds at a bulk store). Wash the outside of each pumpkin well and broil for 5 minutes in the oven to warm them up. Ladle hot pumpkin soup into each one, leaving some space at the top (about ¾ in / 20 mm). Spoon in croutons and onions and cover with a generous helping of cheese. Broil until cheese is melted and garnish with toasted pumpkin seeds. Serve immediately on a napkin-lined plate.

Serves 6, with leftovers

Chicken Fricot with Sweet Potato Dumplings

For anyone with Acadian heritage, *fricot* is basically chicken soup. It can most certainly be made with other birds or even hare, but chicken is the most traditional. Served simply with chunks of potatoes and onions, the meat is tender and moist. Here I omit the potato and add a small Italian dumpling or agnolotti which works well with the fragrant summer savory that is so pronounced in any fricot. Traditional pasta works well here but I use wonton wrappers for simplicity. I suggest starting with chicken stock, as I like the intense, rich flavour that results, but the Acadians would have used only water.

Chicken Fricot

2 onions, finely chopped
1 stalk celery, finely chopped
1 tbsp (15 mL) dried summer savory
1 tsp (5 mL) dried thyme
2 bay leaves
2 tbsp (30 mL) butter
1 tsp (5 mL) salt
1 tsp (5 mL) pepper
1 x 5-lb (2.2-kg) free-range chicken
10 cups (2.5 L) fresh or low-sodium chicken stock

Sweet Potato Dumplings

1 lb (450 g) sweet potatoes
2 egg yolks
¼ whole nutmeg, grated
¼ cup (60 mL) grated Parmesan cheese
1 tbsp (15 mL) chopped fresh sage
salt and pepper to taste
1 package wonton wraps, 3-in (7.5-cm) square

For the chicken fricot:

In a stockpot that fits the whole chicken nicely, sauté onions, celery, summer savory, thyme and bay leaves in butter for 3 or 4 minutes until onions are translucent. Add salt, pepper and chicken and cover with stock. Top up the stockpot with water if necessary. Bring to a boil and reduce the heat to a simmer. Cook for 90 minutes, until the meat is tender and falling from the carcass.

For a rustic soup: Remove chicken from the pot and pick meat from the bones. Discard bones and skin. Using a ladle, skim the fat that is floating on top of the stockpot and discard. Add meat back into the soup pot and it is ready.

For a finer soup: Remove chicken from the pot and pick meat as directed above. Strain broth and discard all the vegetables and herbs. Refrigerate broth and meat, separately, overnight. The next day the fat will be solid on the top of the broth. Remove it completely. Reheat soup before serving and return meat to the clear, grease-free broth.

For the dumplings:

Bake sweet potatoes, skin-on, in a 350°F (180°C) oven for 45 minutes to 1 hour, or until flesh inside is soft and creamy. Remove and let cool to room temperature on the counter. Cut each sweet potato in half and scoop out flesh into a mixing bowl. Discard skins (or eat them) and add all remaining ingredients to the bowl. Mix well and refrigerate.

Lay out 3 or 4 wonton wraps at a time. Spoon a heaping teaspoon of the filling in the centre of each wrap, then dip your finger in cold water. Run finger along 2 sides of the wrap and then fold over the dumpling to form a triangle. Seal very well using thumb and forefinger.

Poach the dumplings in water or chicken broth until they float. If making a large batch, lay them out on a baking sheet lined with parchment paper or wax paper. Freeze them individually (making sure they do not touch on the sheet), and transfer them to a freezer container once they are frozen solid. They can be cooked from frozen when you need them.

Place two dumplings in the bottom of a heated soup bowl (three if you are really hungry). Ladle a healthy portion of soup over top of dumplings and serve.

Serves 8, with leftovers

Fricot au Lapin des Bois (Braised Wild Rabbit Hot Pot)

Darren Lewis, Chives Canadian Bistro, Halifax, Nova Scotia

Darren has brought Acadian cultural dishes to our menus at Chives since day one. When I decided to write a book about Canadian bistro food from coast to coast, it was obvious that Darren should represent the Acadian people of Eastern Canada with this warm and winter-perfect stew. "The Acadian people were good farmers and fishermen, as well as hunter-gatherers," says Darren, "skills they honed with the help of the native peoples in the region. This recipe is a twist on an old Acadian favourite, traditionally made with wild hare, which they trapped themselves, and with the potatoes in the stew. But I prefer the flavour of the less gamey and more accessible farmed rabbit and to serve the potatoes on the side."

½ cup (125 mL) diced salt-cured pork belly

½ cup (125 mL) flour

1 tsp (5 mL) sea salt

1 tsp (5 mL) freshly ground black pepper

1 wild or farmed rabbit, cut into 8 pieces

2 cups (500 mL) pearl onions

2 carrots, finely diced

2 stalks of celery, finely diced

1 shallot, minced

4 cloves garlic, minced

2 tbsp (30 mL) dried summer savory

1 cup (250 mL) dry white wine

6 cups (1500 mL) chicken broth

Place a ceramic-lined cast iron braising pot over medium-high heat and render salt pork until it is very crisp. Remove from the pan and set aside. Mix flour, salt and pepper together and dredge rabbit pieces in flour. Brown rabbit pieces on all sides in the pork drippings. Remove rabbit and set aside. To the pot, add onions, carrots and celery and sauté for a few minutes until they begin to soften and take some colour, then add shallot, garlic and savory, and sauté for another 5 minutes. Deglaze pot with wine and reduce it by half, then return rabbit pieces to the pot. Pour chicken broth into the pot and bring to the boil.

Cover the braising pot and place in a 300°F (150°C) oven for 1 hour. The meat should be fork-tender. Transfer rabbit pieces to a hot serving platter to keep warm. Using a slotted spoon, remove pearl onions from the broth and set aside. Place braising pan, uncovered, on high heat and let braising liquor reduce until it coats the back of a wooden spoon. Strain sauce through a sieve or china cap and season to taste with salt and pepper. Return pearl onions to strained sauce as an internal garnish.

Presentation:

Place 2 pieces of rabbit on each plate. Ladle some of the sauce over the meat and garnish with the reserved crispy pork belly. Serve with buttered baby red potatoes and haricots verts.

Serves 4

Domus Beetroot Borscht with Smoked Mackerel and Crème Fraîche

John Taylor, Domus Café, Ottawa, Ontario

Beetroot is a common ingredient during the winter. Many northern European cultures once sustained their families with just such root vegetables. This Russian soup is smooth, sweet, and a real treat. Beets seem lighter and more refreshing than other root vegetables in soups and stews, due to their sweetness. Adding some smoked mackerel, crème fraîche and chives gives this dish some balance and makes it into a meal on its own. You can omit the rutabaga and celery root if you like, but they do add a nice flavour base and make the purée less watery.

Soup Base

1 cup (250 mL) diced rutabaga
1 cup (250 mL) diced celery root
1 carrot, peeled and diced
¼ cup (60 mL) canola oil
1 tsp (5 mL) salt
1 tsp (5 mL) black pepper
2 onions, peeled and diced
5 lb (2.2 kg) red beets, peeled and diced
8 cups (2 L) chicken or vegetable stock approximately

Garnish

6 oz (190 g) smoked trout or mackerel, flaked
¼ cup (60 mL) sour cream or crème fraîche
1 tbsp (15 mL) fresh sliced chives

For the soup base:

Stir rutabaga, celery root, carrot and 3 tbsp (45 mL) of oil in a mixing bowl. Season with salt and pepper and toss to mix. Spread vegetables out on a baking tray and roast in a 400°F (200°C) oven for 20 to 30 minutes, or until vegetables begin to caramelize.

Add 1 tbsp (15 mL) of oil to a stockpot, and cook onions until they start to brown. Add caramelized vegetables from the oven along with beets and chicken stock and bring to the boil. The amount of stock used may vary, so just cover with broth and top up with a little water if needed. Simmer until vegetables are very soft. Blend in a high-powered blender and strain through a fine-meshed chinois or sieve.

Presentation:

Heat 6 cups (1.5 L) of soup base. Ladle 1 cup (250 mL) into each large, heated soup bowl. Warm smoked trout or mackerel for a few seconds in a microwave if desired and place a couple of flaked pieces on top of the soup in the centre of the bowl. Garnish with a dollop of sour cream and sliced chives over the top.

Serves 6, with leftovers

Sweet Potato Soup with Warm Mussel, Shiitake and Winter Leek Salad

Soups are an essential part of surviving the Canadian winter. Soup-making is relaxing and comforting. I fancy up this simple, nutritious puréed soup with a warm salad made from steamed mussels, haystack-cultivated shiitake mushrooms and winter leeks from the cold stores, but you can omit this step and serve it as is. Other garnishes I have used in the past include bacon bits and sour cream, roasted peppers with spicy chipotle coulis, and fried onions with croutons and Gruyere.

Soup

1 cup (250 mL) diced celery

1 cup (250 mL) diced onion

3 cloves garlic, coarsely chopped

1 tsp (5 mL) salt

½ tsp (3 ml) freshly ground black pepper

½ tsp (3 mL) dried thyme

½ tsp (3 mL) fennel seeds

½ tsp (3 mL) chili flakes

¼ cup (60 mL) butter

½ cup (125 mL) white wine

4 cups (1 L) peeled and diced sweet potato

6 cups (1.5 L) chicken or vegetable broth

½ cup (125 mL) 35% cream

Salad

1 lb (450 g) mussels

¼ cup (125 mL) white wine or dry vermouth

1 clove garlic, minced

1 shallot, minced

1 cup (250 mL) sliced shiitake mushrooms

½ cup (125 mL) sliced winter leeks, white part only

2 tbsp (30 mL) extra-virgin olive oil

1 tbsp (15 mL) white wine vinegar

1 tsp (5 mL) chopped fresh parsley

salt and pepper to taste

For the soup:

In a pot, sauté celery, onions, garlic and all seasonings and herbs in butter. Cook for 10 minutes over medium heat until a little colour starts to form. Deglaze pot with wine and turn up the heat to boil off all the liquid. Add sweet potatoes and broth and bring to a boil. Reduce the heat and simmer for 1 hour, or until sweet potatoes begin to fall apart. Purée in a high-speed blender and strain through a fine strainer or chinois. Return purée to the soup pot and add cream. Keep on a very low heat until ready to serve.

For the warm salad:

Steam mussels in white wine, garlic and shallot in a covered pot until they just open, about 2 minutes. Begin to sauté mushrooms and leeks in olive oil while you are quickly shucking mussels. Pour juice from mussels into the sauté pan to deglaze, and reduce liquid until only 1 tbsp (15 mL) or so remains. Add shucked mussels to the pan with vinegar and parsley. Remove from the heat immediately and adjust seasonings.

Presentation:

Pour a full ladle of hot soup into a *shallow* soup bowl (the warm salad should be visible and not sink to the bottom). Make a neat pile of salad in the centre of the bowl. Garnish with a sprig of fresh parsley and a mussel shells.

Serves 6, with leftovers

Elegant Split Pea Soup with Smoked Turkey

There are many ways to make split pea soup, but this one is a little different. First of all, I love to use smoked turkey legs I can find at the local butcher, but ham hocks are great if you prefer. The variation here is in the purée. I like my soup velvety smooth, and I also add a few leaves of spinach at the end for a vibrant green colour. So get out your blender. This soup can be served for lunch with a roll or as a starter to a very elegant Saturday night meal with discerning friends.

2 large smoked turkey legs

12 cups (3 L) cold water

2 onions, 1 whole and 1 finely chopped

4 whole cloves

2 stalks celery, 1 whole and 1 finely chopped

1 carrot

3 sprigs fresh thyme

2 bay leaves

1 leek, cleaned and thinly sliced

1 lb (450 g) green split peas, rinsed

1 cup (250 mL) spinach leaves

½ cup (125 mL) 35% cream

salt and pepper to taste

½ cup (125 mL) crème fraîche or sour cream (for garnish)

2 green onion tops, sliced (for garnish)

In a stockpot, place turkey legs and water and bring to a simmer. Stud whole onion with cloves and add to the pot along with whole celery stalk, whole carrot, thyme sprigs and bay leaf. Simmer for 2 hours or until turkey meat is falling off the bone. Carefully remove legs with a slotted spoon and set aside to cool. Remove carrot and the whole onion as well and discard. If the pot has lost some of its liquid through evaporation, top it up with a little water.

Now add diced onion, diced celery, sliced leek and split peas to the pot. Simmer for 90 minutes with the lid on the pot — do not boil or the peas will stick. While the soup simmers, pick meat off the turkey bones and shred into small pieces. Discard bones and reserve the meat.

When peas are soft, add spinach to the soup and immediately begin to purée in a high-speed blender. Pass soup through a sieve or fine-meshed chinois and add a little water if it seems a bit thick. Pour strained soup into a clean soup pot and add cream. Bring back to a simmer and adjust seasonings. Add turkey meat and simmer once again.

Ladle hot soup into soup or consommé bowls (a tea cup with saucer makes a nice presentation as well). Garnish with a dollop of crème fraîche and a couple of slices of green onion tops.

Serves 6, with leftovers

Maritime Seafood Chowder

Michael Smith, Food Network Canada, Fortune, Prince Edward Island

I began my apprenticeship with Michael Smith in 1996. At that time he was the chef at the celebrated Inn at Bay Fortune. My summer with Michael was demanding but, ultimately, the most rewarding and important step of my early career. Michael taught me to cook like a Canadian chef. He was the first person to show me the wonders of growing food for a restaurant and of sourcing local ingredients. Michael has become Canada's most recognized chef, and his food has become incredibly simple yet more rewarding than ever. "The best recipes are always the simplest," he writes, "and this is my favourite for chowder. It's the one I make at home."

8 slices smoky bacon, finely chopped

1 medium cooking onion, finely chopped

2 stalks celery, minced

½ cup (125 mL) dry white wine

1 cup (250 mL) 35 % cream

1 cup (250 mL) milk

2 x 5-oz (140-g) cans baby clams, with juice

2 bay leaves

1 tsp (5 mL) fresh thyme leaves

1 cup (250 mL) grated baking potato

1 ½ lb (675 g) fresh local seafood (whitefish, lobster or whatever you have)

1 x 10-oz (300-mL) can unsweetened evaporated milk (substitute with 35% cream if desired)

¼ cup (60 mL) chopped flatleaf parsley

salt and pepper

In a thick-bottomed soup pot, brown bacon until crisp. Pour off half the fat. Add onion and celery with a splash of water and sauté for a few minutes until soft. Add white wine, cream, milk and juice from the clams (reserve the clam meat). Add bay leaves, thyme and grated potato and bring mixture to a slow simmer. Continue simmering for fifteen minutes until grated potato softens and chowder base thickens. Add reserved clam meat, seafood, evaporated milk and parsley. Bring back to simmer. Taste chowder and season with salt and pepper. Serve immediately with your favourite biscuits.

Serves 4 (with seconds)

Salads & Vegetables

The ingredients and the role of the salad in a meal vary depending upon where you live. In our culture a traditional salad contains a mixed green variety, often accompanied by tomatoes, cucumber and grated carrots. Due to the neutrality of the lettuces, the salad becomes a vehicle for whatever dressing is poured over the top. In Eastern European countries salad usually means simple sliced onions and tomatoes. In France the salad is a course served after the main to aid in digestion. And in Italy the insalate is served before the pasta, often as part of the antipasti course.

But the salad is so much more to a modern chef, and endless combinations can result from the amazing bounty of available ingredients. Bistro salads follow only one rule: the ingredients must be at the peak of freshness — nothing is more important. And although we crave salads in summertime more than in any other season, many great "off-season" salads make restaurant menus vibrant, despite the lack of sunshine. Cured meats, cheeses, root vegetables and preserved items become the focus during these months, along with hothouse produce that continues to provide some greenery as the snow flies.

The chef who cooks seasonally will also create vegetarian dishes that often follow similar themes. The addition of spice, heat and perhaps a side dish can transform a great vegetarian salad, drawn from the same ensemble of ingredients, into a main meal.

In this chapter the important point to note is the seasonal feel of the dishes. Understanding the diversity of Canadian products year round will add great variety to your menus and make eating dinner a healthier and more satisfying experience.

Roasted Shiitake Mushroom Salad with Charred Onions and Asparagus and Basil Anchoiade

Renee Lavallée, Five Fishermen, Halifax, Nova Scotia

When Renee moved to Halifax and took over at the landmark *Five Fishermen Restaurant* a serious buzz erupted in town. Renee's dishes are complex and combine many subtle European and French bistro flavours with our best local seafood and produce. There is a bit of everything in her food, and always the flavours are balanced but striking. In the salad she presents here, the vegetables may seem unassuming and quite ordinary, but when doused with the incredible dressing they become absolutely amazing. *Anchoiade* is an anchovy-based pesto-style sauce, lightened here with basil leaves. I guarantee you will make this dish more than once.

Roasted Mushrooms

1 lb (450 g) fresh shiitake mushrooms, cleaned and stems
  removed if very woody
½ cup (125 mL) olive oil
3 cloves garlic (peeled and crushed with the back of a knife)
6 sprigs fresh thyme, leaves picked
½ tsp (3 mL) salt
½ tsp (3 mL) freshly ground black pepper

Charred Onions and Asparagus

1 bunch asparagus
1 red onion, sliced into ½-in (1-cm) rings
1 white onion, sliced into ½-in (1-cm) rings
3 tbsp (45 mL) olive oil
salt and pepper to taste

Basil Anchoiade

1 cup (250 mL) basil leaves, cleaned and roughly torn
1 clove garlic
4 anchovy fillets
1 cup (250 mL) extra-virgin olive oil
zest and juice of 1 lemon
salt and pepper to taste
¼ cup (60 mL) grated Parmesan cheese

For the roasted mushrooms:

Preheat oven to 400°F (200°C) and place mushrooms on a baking tray, ensuring they are not too crowded. Drizzle with olive oil, garlic, thyme, salt and pepper and mix well, using your hands to coat everything. Roast for 15 to 20 minutes, or until soft. Stir occasionally to ensure even cooking. Set aside until ready to use

For the onion and asparagus:

Wash asparagus well and remove bottom 1 ½ to 2 in (4 to 5 cm) as that part can be woody and unpleasant to eat. Preheat grill or barbecue on high. Toss asparagus and onions separately with olive oil and seasonings. Grill onions first and cook until soft and well charred. Next add asparagus (these take only a minute, so keep an eye on them). Set vegetables aside to cool.

For the anchoiade:

In a blender, place basil, garlic and anchovies. Start to process while slowly adding olive oil. Add lemon zest and juice, check for seasonings and add as desired. Continue to process and check seasoning again. Adjust if necessary with more oil or lemon juice. Finish by adding Parmesan cheese and give one last pulse in the blender (anchoiade should have a thick consistency).

To assemble, mix together roasted mushrooms, charred onions and asparagus, again checking for seasonings, and place on a plate. Drizzle with some anchoiade and a little black pepper to finish.

Serves 6 to 8

Salad Niçoise

Great year-round salads are often hard to find if you are focused on sourcing local ingredients — pickings are slim in winter and early spring. I love this salad because it is flexible throughout the year. When I can use fresh tuna, just seared and thinly sliced, with heirloom tomatoes and garden greens, great. In winter canned tuna is usually in the pantry, and I use wonderful greenhouse hydroponic lettuces, tomatoes, fingerling potatoes and globe artichokes, canned each fall, and I usually just skip the green bean element. Free-range eggs, olives and greenhouse herbs are in my kitchen all the time. This salad makes a wonderful meal with some very good bread and a crisp white wine.

6 free-range eggs, hardboiled (9 minutes), peeled, chilled
  and sliced in half.
1 lb (450 g) greenhouse or garden lettuce (such as Boston,
  bibb or mesclun mix)
8 fingerling potatoes, cooked and sliced lengthwise
½ greenhouse English cucumber
1 small red onion, thinly sliced
8 oz (225 g) green beans, blanched in boiling water and
  chilled
2 greenhouse tomatoes, sliced
1 pint (475 mL) greenhouse cherry tomatoes, mixed colours
2 stalks celery, peeled and sliced on the bias
1 cup (250 mL) canned or preserved artichokes, sliced
¾ cup (185 mL) Niçoise olives (Kalamata are fine)
2 x 6-oz (170-g) cans tuna in water
½ cup (125 mL) fresh basil leaves
¾ cup (180 mL) Vinaigrette (recipe follows)

Vinaigrette
3 anchovy fillets
1 shallot, very finely minced
1 clove garlic, minced to a fine pulp
2 tsp (10 mL) Dijon mustard
juice and zest of 1 lemon
1 tbsp (15 mL) white wine vinegar
½ tsp (3 mL) salt
½ tsp (3 mL) freshly ground black pepper
½ cup (125 mL) extra-virgin olive oil

For the salad:
It is best served on a large platter and shared "family style" with everybody helping themselves. Simply lay the greens on the platter and build the salad up from there, garnishing with slices of potatoes, cucumbers, tomatoes, artichokes, olives and crumbled tuna. Fresh basil leaves and a generous bath of vinaigrette is all you need for this simple rustic salad.

Serves 6

For the vinaigrette:
Smash anchovy fillets in a bowl with a fork and add shallot and garlic. Add mustard, lemon juice, lemon zest, vinegar, salt and pepper and whisk until smooth. Add olive oil in a slow, steady stream until vinaigrette is smooth and emulsified. For a larger salad simply double ingredients. Leftover dressing will keep for a couple of weeks in the refrigerator.

Yields ¾ cup (180 mL)

Spinach Ravioli with Morel, Ramp and Mascarpone Sauce

A simple spinach and ricotta filling in freshly made pasta is a bistro — or more specifically an Italian trattoria — classic. Spring spinach, fresh from local fields or greenhouses, gives a much finer flavour than frozen. But the morels and ramps in this recipe are the real showstoppers. Fresh morels have been a B.C. commodity for a very long time, but dried ones are also a good choice in this recipe. Ramps, or wild leeks, are quite common at farmers' markets each spring. They are cooked much like green onions and have a more pronounced garlicky punch. This is a vegetarian dish that will amaze you with its complex flavours and leave you feeling satisfied and inspired by spring.

Pasta
1 lb (450 g) flour
2 eggs plus 4 egg yolks
¼ tsp (1 mL) salt

Filling
8 oz (225 g) fresh spinach leaves
1 cup (250 mL) fresh ricotta cheese
¼ whole nutmeg, freshly grated
1 egg yolk (second amount)
½ tsp (3 mL) sea salt
¼ tsp (1 mL) ground black pepper
2 tbsp (30 mL) grated Parmesan cheese

Morel, Ramp and Mascarpone Sauce
1 shallot, minced
1 ½ cups (375 mL) morel mushrooms (fresh or re-hydrated dried)
4 stalks fresh ramps (wild leeks), sliced
2 tbsp (30 mL) butter
1 clove garlic, minced
2 oz (60 mL) cognac or brandy
½ cup (125 mL) water
¾ cup (185 mL) Mascarpone cheese
3 leaves fresh sage, finely chopped
salt and pepper to taste
½ pint greenhouse cherry tomatoes (for garnish)

For the filling:

Pile flour in the middle of work surface and make a well in the centre. Combine eggs, yolks and salt in the well and, using a fork, begin whisking. Slowly incorporate flour from the sides of the well into the mix. When mixture becomes too thick for the fork, use your hands, and knead dough for 3 or 4 minutes until it is smooth. (It may not be necessary to use all the flour. Weather conditions and varieties of flour make a big difference.) Wrap dough in plastic film and set in the refrigerator for a minimum of 2 hours before use (overnight is best).

Cook spinach in boiling water for 45 seconds and plunge immediately into iced water. Squeeze out water as best you can and chop spinach into small pieces, using a large chef's knife. This can also be done by pulsing spinach in a food processor. Add spinach to a bowl along with ricotta, nutmeg, egg yolk, seasonings, and Parmesan cheese. Mix well and place in a piping bag with a large circular tip (not a star or the filling will clog the tip).

For the pasta:

Using a commercial pasta machine, roll out rested pasta dough using the finest setting on the thickness dial. Follow the instructions for your machine if you are unfamiliar with it. Most machines come with a simple ravioli press that makes 12 raviolis per batch. Place 1 sheet of pasta onto the press, pipe a small amount of filling into each depression, and then lay a second rolled pasta sheet over the top. Repeat the process until pasta and filling are used up. The ravioli can be frozen by laying them onto a baking tray lined with wax paper or parchment. Once they are individually frozen they can be removed from the tray and placed into any freezer container or freezer bag.

Bring 3 gallons of well-salted water to a rolling boil. Cook ravioli for 3 minutes, or until they float. They will take 1 minute longer if cooked from frozen.

Serve about 7 or 8 pieces as an entree, less as an appetizer, with a large spoonful of Morel, Ramp and Mascarpone Sauce. Garnish with cherry tomatoes.

Serves 6 as an appetizer, 4 as a main course

For the sauce:

Sauté shallot, morels and ramps in butter for 3 minutes. Add garlic and flambé with brandy. Reduce brandy and add water and Mascarpone. Stir together and add sage and seasonings.

Buffalo Mozzarella, Heirloom Tomato and Polenta Salad

Rob Fracchioni, Millcroft Inn and Spa, Caledon, Ontario

Chef Fracchioni's food at the Millcroft Inn showcases Ontario-grown, seasonal produce. Herbs are picked from the restaurant garden just prior to preparation. When you read the menu you see Italy, France and Switzerland represented in elegant touches, but the Canadian feel is most pronounced. Roberto explores his Italian heritage with the lovely salad he offers here. He makes use of my favourite summer vegetable (or fruit, to be precise), the heirloom tomato. Use Kalamata olives if you can't find the Italian varieties. You can also substitute bocconcini cheese for the fresh mozzarella.

Polenta

2 cups (500 mL) water
½ tsp (3 mL) sea salt
½ cup (125 mL) fine to medium cornmeal
a few grindings of black pepper
1 tbsp (15 mL) butter
2 tbsp (30 mL) grated Parmesan cheese
olive oil for grilling

Stuffed Tomatoes

6 heirloom tomatoes, about 2 ½ in (6 cm) in diameter
1 piece (about 3 ½ oz, 100 g) buffalo milk mozzarella,
   coarsely grated or hand-shredded
⅓ cup (85 mL) Taggiasche olives, coarsely chopped
2 tbsp (30 mL) Bella di Cerignola olives, coarsely chopped
1 sprig fresh oregano, leaves picked and chopped
4 leaves fresh basil, chopped
2 cloves garlic, minced
salt and pepper

Pancetta Crisp Garnish

6 slices round pancetta

Salad

3 cups (750 mL) baby arugula leaves
2 tsp (10 mL) red wine vinegar
2 tbsp (30 mL) good olive oil
1 tbsp (15 mL) grapeseed oil
a pinch of salt and pepper

For the polenta:

In a heavy-bottomed pot bring water and salt to a boil. Reduce to a simmer and slowly whisk in cornmeal. Then use a wooden spoon to stir polenta over very low heat for 30 to 40 minutes. Season with pepper and stir in butter and cheese. Pour onto a tray lined with parchment paper to a thickness of about ½ in (1 cm). Allow to cool completely so polenta is firm to the touch. Cut into 6 rounds with a 2 ½- to 3-in (6- to 7.5-cm) cookie cutter. Preheat barbecue grill and brush polenta cakes with a little olive or grapeseed oil. Grill for 1 minute on each side, marking cakes with a crosshatched design. Set aside on the lined tray again until ready to serve.

For the tomatoes:

Cut off top of each tomato about ½ in (1 cm) from top, exposing seeds. Cut a very small slice from the bottom of each tomato as well so it stands up straight, but be careful not to cut too deep. With a melon baller or teaspoon, remove seeds and pulp of tomato, making sure not to break through the sides. Discard seeds but reserve the more fleshy tomato "meat." Turn hollowed-out tomatoes upside down on paper towels to drain out any liquid.

   Coarsely chop removed tomato "meat" and add it to a bowl with mozzarella cheese, olives, herbs and garlic. Season the inside of each hollowed tomato with a little salt and pepper and stuff with olive and cheese mixture. Replace tomato tops and rest tomatoes on the same tray as polenta.

For the pancetta crisp garnish:

Place sliced pancetta on a flat baking tray lined with parchment paper. Place another layer of parchment on top of pancetta. Place another flat oven tray on top of pancetta to keep them flat while they cook. (This technique works best if you have two baking trays that rest tightly in each other).

   Place in a 300°F (150°C) oven and cook for 7 to 15 minutes, turning the tray in the oven often, until pancetta is crispy. Watch very carefully as it will burn easily. Remove from the tray and set aside on some paper towel to absorb any excess fat, allowing pancetta to become crisp.

For the salad:

Toss arugula with vinegar and oils, seasoning with salt and pepper to taste.

Presentation:

Warm grilled polenta pucks and stuffed tomatoes in a 350°F (180°C) oven for 5 minutes. Place a small pile of dressed arugula in the centre of each serving plate. Nestle a warm polenta disk on top of greens and place tomato on top of polenta. An additional garnish of fresh basil can be added if desired. Lean pancetta crisp against tomato and serve.

Serves 6

BLT Salad with Fried Red Fife Wheat Bread, Just-poached Egg and Tarragon Mayo Vinaigrette

Each year I try a few new twists on summer salads using heirloom tomatoes, and everything is just that much better topped off with a runny, poached free-range egg. One can hardly imagine a bistro without a fresh summer salad and a loaf of perfect bread, a symbol of sharing and family. Red Fife is a heritage variety of wheat that, at its peak, fed Canadians in the west for decades. Production fell off, then in 2003 a few people involved in the International Slow Food movement here in Canada nominated Red Fife wheat for the *Ark of Taste*. Production has steadily increased since then and more and more Canadians are falling in love with this delicious heritage grain. I present a simple loaf of bread below for you to try, whether you make the salad or not.

Red Fife Wheat Bread

¼ cup (60 mL) honey

1 cup plus 2 tbsp (280 mL) warm water

2 tsp (10 mL) active dry yeast

3 tbsp (45 mL) bread flour

3 tbsp (45 mL) ground flax

2 tbsp (30 mL) quinoa

½ tsp (3 mL) salt

2 cups (500 mL) Red Fife wheat flour (plus another ½ cup/ 125 mL or so for kneading)

¼ cup (60 mL) vegetable oil

1 tbsp (15 mL) butter (optional)

Tarragon Mayo Vinaigrette

1 cup (250 mL) real mayonnaise

¼ cup (60 mL) tarragon vinegar

¼ cup (60 mL) water

1 tbsp (15 mL) honey

1 tsp (5 mL) Dijon mustard

1 tbsp (15 mL) chopped fresh tarragon

½ tsp (3 mL) salt

a few dashes of Tabasco or other hot sauce

Salad

8 slices good smoked bacon

6 mixed red, yellow or orange heirloom tomatoes

3 green zebra tomatoes

2 cups (500 mL) mixed grape or cherry tomatoes

2 heads red- or green-leaf field lettuce (any variety will do)

1 clove garlic

6 tbsp (90 mL) extra-virgin olive oil

8 small slices Red Fife Wheat Bread, cut ½-in (1-cm) thick

1 tsp (5 mL) white vinegar

8 eggs

For the bread:

Mix honey and water together and sprinkle yeast over the top. Wait until yeast begins to activate and foam. In a larger mixing bowl, combine bread flour, flax, quinoa, salt and 2 cups (500 mL) Red Fife flour. Add yeast and water, then the oil, and mix to form a dough. Remove from the bowl and place on a clean work surface sprinkled with some of the extra flour. Knead until a smooth, elastic dough forms. Depending on the humidity you may need a bit more flour for kneading.

Cover dough and let rise in a warm place until doubled in size. Punch dough down again, knead into a ball, and form into a cylinder about 8 in (20 cm) long. Allow the loaf to rise a second time until doubled in size. This should take about 30 minutes if left in a warm place. Preheat oven to 375°F (190°C) and bake on the middle rack for 25 to 35 minutes. Remove from the oven and rub top of crust with butter while hot.

For the vinaigrette:

Simply combine all ingredients in a bowl and mix very well until smooth and creamy. For a thinner or thicker dressing, adjust water a little.

For the salad:

Lay bacon on a baking tray and cook in a 350°F (180°C) oven for 12 to 15 minutes until crispy and dark golden brown. Remove and set on a plate lined with clean paper towel to remove any excess fat. Set aside, as bacon can be served at room temperature for this salad.

Cut tomatoes in a variety of shapes (thick slices, wedges, or smaller ones in half) and clean lettuce. Slice garlic clove into 2 or 3 pieces, and place in a large frying pan with olive oil. Over medium heat (not so hot that the garlic burns) fry bread until golden brown, as you would for a grilled cheese sandwich. Keep bread warm in the pan while you poach eggs.

Bring 4 quarts (4L) of water to a boil and add vinegar. Bring to a simmer and poach eggs for 4 minutes. Remove from water with a slotted spoon just before you serve salads. (Note: This should be done once salads are almost fully plated and ready to serve so that the eggs do not overcook.)

Presentation:

Make a bed of lettuce and mix tomatoes, bread and broken bacon strips (2 half slices per person) together. Pile loosely on top of lettuce, place an egg on each and drizzle a couple of tablespoons of tarragon mayo over the top. Using a small paring knife, slit egg yolk and allow it to run down into the salad for an extra "wow" factor. Serve while egg is warm.

Serves 8

Flageolets with Carrots and Sauce Soubise

Jamie Kennedy, JK Gardiner Museum, Toronto, Ontario

I remember making Sauce Soubise in culinary school. I thought at the time that sauces needed reductions, demi-glace, cream and days of organization and prep work. But the more you cook and gain a better understanding of the properties of food, the more you can cast aside expectations of what great cooking is and focus on the flavours that already exist in our food. An onion is often all you need to make a dish perfect. Chef Kennedy understands this and enjoys bringing a few simple but perfect vegetables together on a plate. He uses beautiful heirloom carrots (purple, yellow, and orange) that bring color and life to this elegant vegetarian bistro dish. It can be served on its own or as a side dish.

Flageolets with Carrots

½ lb (225 g) freshly shucked flageolet beans
1 clove garlic, thinly sliced
12 pearl onions, peeled
4 carrots, various heirloom varieties, scrubbed and sliced thickly on the bias
1 bay leaf
1 sprig fresh thyme
salt to taste
pat of butter (optional)

Sauce Soubise

4 medium-sized onions, peeled and thinly sliced
½ lb (225 g) butter
sea salt and pepper to taste
1 tsp (5 mL) apple cider vinegar (or to taste)

For the flageolets:

Place all ingredients except salt in a large saucepan. Cover with cold water and bring to a boil. Reduce to a simmer and cook for approximately 30 minutes. Strain off any remaining water, season to taste with salt and add a small pat of butter if desired.

For the sauce:

Place sliced onions and butter in a saucepan and cook slowly until onions are transparent but not browned. This should take about 30 minutes. Transfer to a blender and process to a smooth purée. Season with salt and a touch of cider vinegar.

Presentation:

Warm an oval ceramic serving dish in the oven. Pour some Sauce Soubise into the dish. Spoon bean and carrot mixture on top. Serve immediately.

Serves 4 to 6

Mushroom and Ricotta Toast

The best way to enjoy this dish is to use the barbecue, especially if you have a side burner attachment. The mushrooms here are absolutely essential. Do not use button mushrooms for this recipe as their subtle flavour will be lost. This recipe is meant to showcase the very best wild mushrooms you can find. I have suggested a few varieties, but use whatever you can find at the market. Grilling the bread gives a fantastic flavour that works well with the smooth cheese and aromatic mushrooms. Do not be afraid to let some charred edges develop. This is a surprisingly delicious appetizer or lunch dish.

3 tbsp (45 mL) extra-virgin olive oil

2 cloves garlic, minced

1 cup (250 mL) sliced chanterelle mushrooms

1 cup (250 mL) sliced king oyster mushrooms

1 cup (250 mL) sliced shiitake mushrooms

1 cup (250 mL) sliced black trumpet mushrooms

1 tsp (5 mL) chopped sage leaves

2 or 3 sprigs thyme, leaves picked

½ tsp (3 mL) salt

freshly ground black pepper

2 tbsp (30 mL) water

2 tbsp (30 mL) salted butter

4 slices French baguette or sourdough bread (something with a crust)

2 tbsp (30 mL) extra-virgin olive oil (second amount)

1 cup (250 mL) creamy ricotta cheese

Preheat barbecue and side burner. Sauté garlic in olive oil for 1 minute and add mushrooms. Cook for 3 minutes on high heat then add chopped sage, thyme and seasonings. When mushrooms are slightly brown, add water and cook for 1 more minute. Finally, remove from the heat, add butter and stir into mushrooms. The butter will help bind the flavourful liquid at the bottom of the pan. Set aside for 2 minutes.

Brush baguette slices with olive oil on both sides and grill until toasted to your liking. Divide cheese and spread evenly on the bread. Spoon mushrooms over each piece of bread and serve immediately.

Serves 4

Grilled Pear, Prosciutto and Goat's Cheese Fritter Salad

Ross and Simon Fraser, Fraser Café, Ottawa, Ontario

In early autumn, almost all the wonderful salad vegetables and field lettuces we find in the summer, with the exception of some young lettuces, are still available for great salads. Tomatoes are ripe and ready, and our appetites are still ready for lighter summer fare. But by the middle or end of autumn we begin to see "warmer" salads appear — those that use orchard fruit and items from cold storage. Warmth can also be added with actual heat. This salad introduces warm or cooked elements to a refreshing salad and pairs classic ingredients like pears and prosciutto. Frisée lettuce can be replaced here with any other tart, peppery lettuce like chicory or radicchio.

Honey-Vinegar Dressing
¼ cup + 1 tbsp (75 mL) liquid honey
½ cup (125 mL) quality sherry vinegar
¼ cup (60 mL) olive oil
toasted and freshly cracked black pepper to taste
pinch of salt

Fritters
9 oz (250 g) fresh goat's cheese
½ tsp (3 mL) freshly cracked black pepper
3 tbsp (45 mL) mixed chopped herbs, such as parsley, dill and tarragon
¼ cup (60 mL) flour
2 eggs, beaten (for breading)
½ cup (125 mL) panko bread crumbs
2 cups (500 mL) canola oil
sea salt to taste

Salad
3 unpeeled pears, each cut into 8 segments
2 tbsp (30 mL) olive oil
2 cups (500 mL) frisée lettuce
1 cup (250 mL) baby arugula leaves
⅓ cup (85 mL) Honey-Vinegar Dressing (recipe above)
¼ cup (60 mL) shallots, minced
3 oz (100 g) thinly sliced prosciutto (about 6 slices)
a few sprigs of fresh herbs
salt and pepper to taste

For the dressing:
Combine all ingredients in a bowl and whisk together.

For the fritters:
In a bowl, mix goat's cheese, freshly ground pepper and herbs together. Form into 1-oz (30-g) disks, roughly 3/8-in (1-cm) thick, using your hands to compress the cheese. Dredge each disk in flour, patting off the excess. Dip disks into beaten egg and then into breadcrumbs. You can repeat the egg and breadcrumb step to form a thicker crust.

   (Note: Do not complete the next step until just before you are ready to serve the salad.) Heat oil in a shallow frying pan (use a home deep fryer if you prefer) and fry fritters until golden brown. Remove from oil, and sprinkle with sea salt while still hot.

For the salad:
Preheat barbecue. Drizzle pear segments lightly with olive oil and grill for approx 1 to 2 minutes per side. In a bowl, toss together greens with a generous amount of the Honey-Vinegar Dressing and shallots.

Presentation:
Start with a pile of dressed greens and slices of prosciutto in the centre of a large plate. Lay grilled pear segments (about 4 per person) and a fritter on top. Garnish with fresh herbs and some cracked black pepper. Serve warm.

Serves 6

Sea Scallop, Pickled Beet and Goat's Cheese Salad with Maple Buttermilk Dressing

I have used pickled beets in several variations over the years, but they most often appear on my early spring menu in a salad. Although spring may have "sprung" on the calendar, very little is growing in March or April, except in greenhouses. You might call this a pantry salad, as it uses ingredients I typically have in my larder. Most importantly though, it is a delicious and well-balanced salad with lots of sweetness, acidity and crunch — the three keys to a great salad course. The addition of properly seared sweet sea scallops is a great way to fancy this up, but it is equally enjoyable as a vegetarian dish.

Pickled Red and Golden Beets

3 lb (1.3 kg) golden beets
3 lb (1.3 kg) red beets
4 cups (1 L) white wine vinegar
4 cups (1 L) apple cider vinegar
4 cups (1 L) sugar
1 tbsp (15 mL) mustard seeds
8 bay leaves
1 tbsp (15 mL) black pepper corns
12 whole cloves

Maple Buttermilk Dressing

¼ cup (60 mL) maple syrup
½ cup (125 mL) buttermilk
¼ cup (60 mL) sour cream
2 tbsp (30 mL) white wine vinegar
2 tbsp (30 mL) light olive oil
1 tbsp (15 mL) chopped fresh chives
¼ tsp (1 mL) salt
1 dash Tabasco sauce
a few grindings of fresh black pepper

Salad

1 cup (250 mL) each of Pickled Red and Golden Beets
2 cups (500 mL) greenhouse mâche lettuce
⅓ cup (85 mL) crumbled fresh goat's cheese
⅓ cup (85 mL) toasted pecans
2 green onion tops, sliced
2 tbsp (30 mL) canola oil
12 large sea scallops (under 10 per pound count)
½ tsp (3 mL) coarse sea salt or fleur de sel
½ cup (125 mL) Maple Buttermilk Dressing

For the pickled beets:

Peel beets and slice them using a mandolin or the slicing attachment of a food processor. The slices should be no more than ⅛-in (3-mm) thick. Place golden and red beet slices in separate 1-L mason jars. Bring all other ingredients to a boil and pour over sliced beets in the jars. Place new mason jar lids on each bottle. For those you intend to store for future use, boil the jars in water, sealed, for 10 minutes to sterilize them.

Yields 6 x 500 mL mason jars (3 red and 3 golden)

For the dressing:

Simply combine all ingredients in a bowl and mix with a whisk until smooth.

For the salad:

Lay out alternating golden and red beets in a straight line about 8 in (20 cm) long (about 4 slices of each). Cover beets with a layer of mâche leaves. Sprinkle crumbled goat's cheese on top of lettuce along with the pecans and green onion slices.

Heat a cast iron, stainless steel or aluminum frying pan over high heat. Add oil and sear scallops on each side for 2 minutes (smaller scallops require less time per side). Properly cooked scallops should be only slightly warm in the centre. Sprinkle with sea salt.

To serve, place 3 scallops on salad and drizzle a couple of tablespoons of Maple Buttermilk Dressing over the top. Serve immediately while scallops are still warm.

Serves 4

Hot & Cold Appetizers

There is probably no other part of the bistro menu that provides as much opportunity for creativity as the appetizer list. Forget the chicken wings, nacho platter and spring rolls for a moment. As delicious as these dishes may be, the great bistros and restaurants of today tend to observe a more distinctly Canadian cultural influence in their starting dishes. Crunchy fishcakes, smoked salmon, simply prepared seafood, charcuterie meats and excellent cheeses are the focus, to name but a few. The influences of our European backgrounds are also seen in these recipes, but the ingredient base is truly Canadian. Excluding the obvious soup and salad options that begin a meal, chefs can build great multi-course menus from a wide variety of appetizers that can be healthy as well as exciting and flavourful.

The other great bonus to having a collection of "go to" appetizer recipes is the speed with which they can be transformed into lunchtime options. Whether in a bistro or at home, add a salad to many of these dishes and they will keep you going until suppertime.

The "Canadian bistro" collection of appetizers that follow is a mixture: some of these dishes are very simple and others are somewhat challenging. The ingredient base is quite small for each, but the recipes attempt to show you how to properly prepare interesting dishes rooted in classical cooking. So get ready to confit, sauté and blend your way to a great dinner party, just as the chefs in your local bistro do every day.

Lobster Gnudi with Beurre Fondue

Michael Moffatt, Beckta, Ottawa, Ontario

Gnudi are small Italian dumplings like *gnocchi* but made with ricotta cheese instead of potato. The cheese requires no cooking so is less time-consuming, and the result is a soft and perfect little morsel. Michael served me a version of this dish and summed it up perfectly. "It tastes like the fried cheese that hits the pan when making a grilled cheese sandwich," he said. Nutty, rich and luxurious, this dish is a wonderful starter, and it highlights the sweet lobster flavour. The interesting sauce is really just the poaching liquid for the lobster, an emulsified liquid butter that does not hide the flavours of the sea contained in the flesh of the meat.

Gnudi

1 egg
¾ lb (340 g) fresh ricotta cheese
¼ lb (115 g) freshly grated Parmesan cheese
¼ tsp (1 mL) salt
a pinch of freshly grated black pepper
⅓ cup (85 mL) semolina flour
1 tbsp (15 mL) all-purpose flour
2 tbsp (30 mL) butter (for sautéing gnudi before serving)

Butter-poached Lobster

1 lobster (1 ½ to 2 lb, 675 to 900 g) or 8 oz (225 g) raw
   lobster meat
4 tbsp (60 mL) water
1 cup (125 mL) salted butter
chives or tarragon leaves for garnish

For the gnudi:

In a small mixing bowl, combine egg, ricotta, Parmesan, salt, pepper, all-purpose flour and ½ the semolina flour. Mix until ingredients are well combined.

Place remaining semolina flour in a shallow bowl. Using floured hands, pinch about 1 tbsp (15 mL) of ricotta mixture and form into a little football shape. Repeat, dredging each dumpling through flour in the bowl then placing it onto a baking sheet. Blanch dumplings in simmering water for 2 minutes or until they float. Transfer carefully to a sheet pan and refrigerate until firm.

Heat a frying pan over medium heat and sauté cold gnudi (just removed from the fridge) in butter.

For the lobster:

Cube cold butter into ½-in (1-cm) pieces. Heat water until it just boils in a stainless steel saucepan. Begin adding butter, in pieces, whisking continuously. The butter will emulsify with the water and create a foamy sauce. Do this over a very low heat, as sauce will separate if it boils. When butter is all emulsified, add lobster pieces and poach in the beurre fondue for 5 minutes until just cooked through. If using partially cooked lobster meat from a recently cooked live lobster, the meat will need less time.

Place about 10 pieces of gnudi per person in the centre of a soup or pasta bowl. Place warm lobster on top, followed by a few teaspoons of beurre fondue. Garnish with some sliced chives or a few leaves of fresh tarragon.

Serves 4 to 6, as an appetizer

Duck Cakes with Root Vegetable Ketchup

Moe Mathieu, Willow on the Wascana, Regina, Saskatchewan

Here is a wonderfully simple recipe that uses duck confit. If you do not have the two days required to make it yourself but want to try the cakes, Quebec duck confit is available in many good food markets. The very interesting Root Vegetable Ketchup garnish shows Chef Moe's sense of humour in his bistro cooking. However, this condiment is sweet and tangy and goes perfectly well with the crisp cakes. If you make a large batch it keeps well for a couple of weeks and can be paired with other dishes like roast pork or halibut, or even spread on a hamburger.

Duck Cakes

8 oz (225 g) pulled Duck Confit meat (recipe follows)

8 oz (225 g) warm hand-mashed potatoes (so they are still a bit lumpy)

2 tbsp (30 mL) chopped fresh chives

2 free-range eggs

3 oz (100 g) fresh wholewheat or white breadcrumbs

a tiny pinch of sea salt

¼ tsp (1 mL) freshly ground black pepper

3 tbsp (45 mL) seasoned flour

1 egg, beaten

3 oz (100 g) dry breadcrumbs

¼ cup (60 mL) duck fat

½ tsp (3 mL) fleur de sel (flaky sea salt)

Root Vegetable Ketchup

1 cup (250 mL) white vinegar

1 cup (250 mL) white sugar

1 tsp (5 mL) salt

2 tsp (10 mL) whole allspice

4 whole cloves

2 whole cinnamon sticks

1 cup (250 mL) finely chopped onion

2 cloves garlic, minced

¼ tsp (1 mL) crushed chili flakes

zest of 1 lime

1 beetroot

1 parsnip

1 carrot

Duck Confit

6 tbsp (90 mL) coarse or kosher salt

4 bay leaves, finely crushed

1 tsp (5 mL) powdered clove

1 tsp (5 mL) crushed star anise

1 tsp (5 mL) cracked black peppercorns

6 duck legs

3 lb (1.3 kg) duck fat

2 sprigs sage

2 sprigs thyme

1 sprig rosemary

For the duck cakes:

In a stainless steel bowl, place duck meat, warm mashed potatoes, chives, eggs, fresh breadcrumbs, salt and pepper. Mix well. Form into 2-oz (60-g) balls and gently pat down to form "hockey puck" shapes, with a flat top and bottom and straight sides. Gently roll cakes in seasoned flour, then beaten egg, then dry breadcrumbs, and pat crumbs onto the surface.

Sear cakes in duck fat over medium heat until golden brown on all sides. Sprinkle a little fleur de sel on each cake and serve with Root Vegetable Ketchup.

Yields 18 small cakes

For the ketchup:

In a saucepan, combine all ingredients except the 3 root vegetables. Bring to a simmer, reducing liquid until only 1 cup (250 mL) remains. Blend thoroughly in a standup blender and strain. Reserve ketchup base until needed.

Stab each root vegetable a couple times with a fork, then lay them on a bed of coarse salt and cover with tinfoil. Cook at 300°F (150°C) until all vegetables are fork-tender (about 45 minutes) then peel skins while still warm. Place in a blender and purée with 1 tbsp (15 mL) of ketchup base. Keep adding more base, blending and tasting until you get the flavour and texture you are looking for, but expect to use at least 4 or 5 tbsp (60 or 75 mL). The base can be refrigerated for future use, or a larger batch of finished ketchup can be made immediately. The shelf life will be shorter once the vegetables are added.

Yields 3 cups

For the duck confit:

Mix salt and dry spices together and rub mixture into duck legs. Place legs on a resting rack and cure, refrigerated, for 6 hours. Brush off spices and rinse thoroughly under cold running water, then pat dry with paper towels. In a saucepan, melt duck fat until just warm. Place duck legs in a lasagna or casserole dish so that they fit snugly in the bottom. Place sage, thyme and rosemary in fat with the legs and cook gently over very low heat for about 2 hours, or until meat is fork-tender. To store confit, simply allow fat to congeal around legs in the refrigerator. You can keep the legs for up to 6 weeks like this in the fridge.

Yields about 1 lb (450 g) of picked meat

Crispy Seasonal Mushroom and Camembert Strudel with Okanagan Cherry, Hazelnut Oil and Baby Green Salad

Ned Bell, Cabana Bar and Grille, Okanagan Valley, British Columbia

Ned Bell is a culinary star on the west coast and has been creating great Canadian cuisine for a long time. In his newest restaurant, Cabana Bar and Grille, a wood-fired forno oven takes centre stage in the kitchen, and the menu reflects that. There are subtle hints of chili and lime for that Southwestern feel, Italian pizzas and aioli and French *bouillabaisse*. But as always, Ned is passionate about the produce and proteins of the area around him, particularly in the Okanagan Valley, his home. In this recipe the chef suggests using Lapin cherries and he will often garnish the strudel with a few extra mushrooms on top.

Strudel

2 ½ lb (1 kg) sautéed assorted mushrooms (crimini, oyster, shiitake, portobello)

¼ cup (60 mL) finely chopped shallots

2 tbsp (30 mL) extra-virgin olive oil

1 tsp (5 mL) salt

½ tsp (3 mL) freshly ground black pepper

¼ cup (60 mL) chopped chives

1 package phyllo pastry, defrosted

1 cup (250 mL) melted butter

½ cup (125 mL) chopped toasted hazelnuts

8 oz (225 g) sliced Camembert cheese

Salad

½ lb (225 g) pitted cherries

3 tbsp (45 mL) balsamic vinegar

2 tbsp (30 mL) hazelnut oil

4 cups (1 L) fresh microgreens or mixed baby lettuces

For the strudel:

Sauté mushrooms with shallots in olive oil until golden brown, season with salt and pepper, and mix in chopped fresh chives while mixture is cooling.

Unwrap phyllo pastry and cover with a damp towel to prevent drying out. Lay out one sheet, brush with melted butter and sprinkle with finely chopped hazelnuts. Cover with another sheet of phyllo and repeat until there are 4 complete layers.

Place mushroom mixture in a long, cylindrical pile across the phyllo pastry, ⅓ of the way onto the sheet. Lay slices of Camembert on top of mushrooms. Fold edge of pastry closest to you over mushrooms and cheese and tuck underneath mushrooms, creating a cylinder. Keeping the cylinder as tight as possible, roll away from you, stopping with only a 1-in (2.5-cm) piece of dough remaining. Brush this edge with a little butter and finish roll. Place roll on a baking sheet with the seam against the pan. Brush roll again with a little more butter.

Bake in a 350°F (180°C) oven for 25 to 30 minutes, until golden brown. Remove from the oven and let stand for 10 minutes. Slice with a bread knife into thick disks and serve with salad and a glass of your favourite chilled Okanagan white or red wine.

Serves 4 to 6

For the salad:

Macerate (marinate) cherries in balsamic vinegar for 30 minutes before assembling salad. In a mixing bowl, toss cherries, vinegar, hazelnut oil and greens together and serve alongside a thick slice of the strudel. You can make the disks as thick or thin as you like, thinner would make for a great appetizer.

Beet and Potato Melt with Cape Vessey Cheese

Jamie Kennedy, Jamie Kennedy Wine Bar, Toronto, Ontario

Even those people with only a remote interest in great Canadian cuisine have heard of Jamie Kennedy. For decades Chef Kennedy has lived and cooked by the mantras that we "up-and-comers" like to think are our own: those of seasonal menus and locally sourced ingredients. Acclamations aside, there are few restaurants in Canada that are more fun to eat in than The Wine Bar. The *little plates* concept that promotes sharing at the table is a wonderfully social way to dine, and a bistro concept in essence. In this dish the Cape Vessey cheese that Jamie uses is a goat's milk cheese from Ontario. Choose a lovely melting sheep's milk cheese or brie if you are looking for a substitute.

8 Dutch fingerling potatoes, about 3 to 4 in (7.5 to 10 cm) in length
4 Candy Cane or other heirloom variety of beet
juice of 3 raw beets
2 shallots, finely diced
2 tbsp (30 mL) cider vinegar
4 oz (120 g) Cape Vessey cheese
one green onion, sliced thinly on the bias

Cook potatoes and beets separately in stainless steel pots until tender (about 30 minutes). Gently simmer beet juice until it has reduced to a syrup (about 20 minutes). Marinate shallots in cider vinegar and set aside. When beets are tender, drain water and let them air dry. While they are still warm, peel and slice them into rounds about ¼ in (5mm) thick. Crosshatch potatoes with a paring knife and "smoosh" them with your thumbs and index finger, as you would for a baked potato. Cut cheese into slices that can be broiled over the potatoes just before serving.

Presentation:

Place beet slices in a circular, overlapping pattern on four plates. Place two potatoes on top of beets. Top with sliced cheese. Place each plate under the broiler until cheese is melted and golden. Remove from broiler and sprinkle with marinated shallots and sliced green onions. Spoon some reduced beet juice onto each plate and serve immediately.

Serves 4, as an appetizer

Smoked Haddock Fishcakes with Celery Root, Apple and Golden Beet Salad

Renee Lavallée, Five Fishermen, Halifax, Nova Scotia

Fishcakes are a very personal item, and many people claim to make the best version. For me fishcakes are comforting cold-weather food, sometimes served with baked beans for a weekend supper. They make great morning brunch with eggs over-easy and green tomato chow, or as Renee presents them here, a lovely lunch or appetizer with a unique coleslaw-inspired salad. You could use any fish for a fishcake but smoked haddock is a great choice for flavour, aroma and affordability. The white truffle oil Renee uses is available at nearly any good grocery store or international food market and will keep for a long time in the fridge.

Fishcakes

1 lb (450 g) smoked haddock
1 lb (450 g) baby red- or yellow-fleshed potatoes
1 tsp (5 mL) sea salt
several grindings of black pepper
juice and zest of 1 lemon
3 tbsp (45 mL) extra-virgin olive oil
½ cup (125 mL) grated Parmesan cheese
4 tbsp (60 mL) chopped fresh tarragon
1 tsp (5 mL) white truffle oil
½ cup (125 mL) canola oil
1 cup (250 mL) panko breadcrumbs (Japanese-style)

Celery Root, Apple and Golden Beet Salad:

1 small celery root, peeled and julienned
1 firm, tart apple (such as Honeycrisp or Jonagold), peeled and julienned
1 golden beet, peeled and julienned
juice and zest of ½ lemon
1 tsp (5 mL) honey
½ cup (125 mL) chopped flatleaf parsley
¼ cup (60 mL) extra-virgin olive oil
salt and pepper to taste

For the fishcakes:

Flake smoked haddock and set aside. Steam or boil potatoes until cooked. Place still-warm potatoes in a stand mixer with paddle and crush slightly, making sure not to overprocess. Add flaked haddock, salt, pepper, lemon juice and zest and mix to combine. Add olive oil while mixing on slow speed until mixture starts to stick together. Add Parmesan, tarragon and truffle oil. Taste for seasoning and add more if you feel that it is needed.

Using an ice cream scoop (2-oz/60-g), form fish mixture into cakes. Pour canola oil into pan and place over high heat. Quickly dip cakes into panko crumbs and place in pan. Cook on one side for 1 ½ minutes, until golden brown, then flip over. Cook for an additional 1 minute, and remove from oil. Place onto a baking tray and into a preheated 400°F (200°C) oven to finish for 3 to 4 minutes.

For the salad:

Mix celery root, apple and beet in a bowl. In a separate bowl, mix together lemon juice and zest, honey, parsley, olive oil and seasonings. Combine with vegetables, mix and marinate for 1 hour before serving.

Serve fishcakes with a large spoonful of salad.

Serves 6

Swiss Capuns (Spaetzle Rolls) with Swiss Chard and Brown Butter

Roland Glauser, Charlotte Lane, Shelburne, Nova Scotia

Chef Roland Glauser and I share a love of Swiss cooking — he grew up there and I apprenticed very near his hometown of Thun. This is a traditional Swiss dish that originates from the region of Graubuenden or Grison, located in the southeast of Switzerland. Swiss heritage is prominent in many parts of Canada, and traditional dishes like spaetzle and rosti are commonplace on Canadian menus, primarily due to European chefs sharing their secrets with us. Decent delis all over our land are now more regularly stocked with once-obscure regional cured and dried meats, such as *Bunderfleish* — Swiss air-dried beef. Think of these little packages as cabbage rolls with an Alpine twist.

Spaetzle Dough

1 ¾ cups (430 mL) sifted flour
½ tsp (3 mL) salt
½ tsp (3 mL) freshly ground black pepper
1 tsp (5 mL) paprika
½ whole nutmeg, freshly grated
3 large eggs
½ cup plus 2 tbsp (155 mL) sparkling water or milk
1/2 cup (125 mL) finely chopped double-smoked bacon
1 onion, finely chopped
½ cup (125 mL) Bunderfleisch or Bresaola, finely diced
1 tbsp (15 mL) chopped parsley
1 tbsp (15 mL) chopped chives
1 tbsp (15 mL) chopped fresh mint
1 tbsp (15 mL) chopped fresh basil

Swiss Chard

2 heads Swiss chard, stems removed, washed (greens only)
chives or green onions for tying the rolls
4 cups (1 L) whole milk
4 cups (1 L) water
1 tbsp (15 mL) salt
2 tbsp (30 mL) chopped fresh mint
½ cup (125 mL) butter
1 cup (250 mL) grated Appenzeller or
   Gruyère cheese

For the spaetzle filling:

In a large bowl, place all ingredients and beat with a whisk until small bubbles appear in the batter. It should be smooth and quite thick in consistency. Sauté bacon in a dry pan until fat renders. Add onions and sauté until caramelized, about 10 minutes over medium heat. Add this mixture, Bunderfleish and chopped herbs into batter, leaving out as much excess fat as possible.

For the swiss chard:

Blanch leaves in well-salted water very briefly and chill them in iced water. Drain and dry on a towel. Fill leaves with a small amount of filling, roll up like a spring roll and tie with a whole chive or green onion strand. Smaller leaves may have to be doubled up and each roll should be about 1 ½ in (4 cm) in diameter and 3 in (7.5 cm) in length.

In a saucepan, combine milk, water, salt and mint and bring to a simmer. Poach each roll in the liquid until the filling is fully cooked and firm (about 160°F / 70°C internal temperature). This should take 10 to 12 minutes. In a second saucepan, melt butter and cook until slightly brown in colour.

Top rolls with a spoonful of browned butter and a liberal amount of grated Swiss cheese. The cheese can be melted in an oven for a minute or two if desired. Serve immediately with a green salad and simple vinaigrette.

Yields 12 to 14 capuns

Atlantic Salmon Tartar

Chris Aerni, Rossmount Inn, St. Andrews By-the-Sea, New Brunswick

Chris Aerni is cooking beautiful and elegant food in New Brunswick. He is an ardent supporter of seasonal and locally sourced ingredients but will use certain key ingredients to add an exotic touch to his dishes. Here he pairs salmon with ripe and rich avocado and essences of the Caribbean for an awesome summer appetizer. "This is a very simple but delicate dish," Chris notes. "The salmon has to be the freshest possible. A good quality extra-virgin olive oil will improve the dish. Only add the lemon juice to the dish seconds before it is served, so no curing of the salmon can occur."

1 x ⅔ lb (300 g) Atlantic salmon fillet

3 ripe avocados

sea salt

ground black pepper

2 tsp (10 mL) rice wine vinegar

4 tsp (20 mL) extra-virgin olive oil

1 tsp (5 mL) fresh chives

1 tsp (5 mL) fresh cilantro

juice of ½ lemon

juice of ½ lime

3 red radishes

Skin salmon fillet and remove all grey parts. Cut into small cubes (the size of a small green pea) and keep refrigerated in a mixing bowl. Cut avocados in half. Remove stones and skins. Cut into cubes the same size as salmon and keep in a separate mixing bowl. Just before serving the dish, season avocados with salt, pepper and rice wine vinegar. Mix well.

Cut chives and cilantro as fine as possible. Season salmon with salt, pepper, extra-virgin olive oil, cilantro and chives. Add lemon and lime juice last. Cut radishes into fine matchsticks.

Presentation:

To finish the dishes, divide avocado and salmon mixtures into six equal parts. Fill a ring mould placed on a plate with avocado mixture, press gently down and top with salmon part. Again press down gently to obtain a straight top. Remove ring mould and garnish with radish.

Serves 6

Beer-braised Crisp Pig Cheeks with Sweet and Sour Tomatoes and Banyuls Gastrique

Steve Vardy, Black Cat Bistro, Ottawa, Ontario

It is a confident chef who can challenge the fundamental way people put food in their mouths. So often, when you are served an entree in a restaurant the meat, starch, vegetable and sauce barely touch on the plate. But when Steve serves this dish, each bite has every element in it, creating a perfectly balanced dish. Cooking the pigs' cheeks is a time-consuming effort but well worthwhile. The result is a sticky and delicious bacon-like appetizer. Banyuls vinegar is tricky to find in some areas of the country, so use a high-quality red-wine or apple-cider vinegar as a substitute.

Pork
1½ lb (675 g) fresh pork cheeks
½ tsp (3 mL) ground cloves
1 tsp (5 mL) coriander seeds
1 tsp (5 mL) fennel seeds
1 tsp (5 mL) green cardamom
1 tsp (5 mL) ground star anise
6 tbsp (90 mL) brown sugar
6 tbsp (90 mL) sea salt
3 tbsp (45 mL) cracked black pepper
¼ cup (60 mL) canola oil
1 onion, coarsely chopped
1 small carrot, coarsely chopped
1 stalk celery, coarsely chopped
4 cloves garlic, sliced
1 bottle (375 mL) of your favourite dark or brown
    microbrewery beer
water or chicken stock, as needed
4 tbsp (60 mL) maple syrup

Sweet and Sour Tomatoes
24 cherry tomatoes, halved
1 shallot, minced
1 tbsp (15 mL) fresh thyme leaves
2 tbsp (30 mL) sugar
1 tbsp (15 mL) salt
½ tsp (3 mL) cracked black pepper
3 tbsp (45 mL) red wine vinegar

Banyuls Gastrique
¼ cup (60 mL) sugar
½ cup (125 mL) Banyuls vinegar
2 tbsp (30 mL) Banyuls wine

Assembly
4 pieces bocconcini cheese (about 2 oz, 60 g each)
¼ cup (60 mL) shaved radish disks
2 tbsp (30 mL) chopped chives
extra-virgin olive oil (for garnishing)
1 cup (250 mL) microgreens or baby lettuce, such as arugula or mâche

For the pork:
Lightly score pork cheeks with a sharp knife and season lightly with salt. Wait for cheeks to sweat. Combine dried spices (cloves, coriander, fennel, cardamom and star anise) and rub into cheeks vigorously.

In a separate bowl combine sugar, salt and pepper. In a nonreactive dish (stainless steel or earthenware) sprinkle ⅓ of salt and sugar mixture and place cheeks on top, skin side up. Sprinkle remaining ⅔ of mixture on top of cheeks and refrigerate for 24 hours.

Remove cheeks from the dish, rinse quickly under cold running water and pat dry with clean towels. Heat some canola oil in a roasting pan, place cheeks skin side down and cook until golden brown. Flip cheeks over and continue to brown, then add onion, carrot, celery and garlic and cook until vegetables are golden brown. Deglaze pork and vegetables in beer and add water or chicken stock just to cover. Cover with parchment paper and cook in a 325°F (165°C) oven for 2 hours.

Remove pork cheeks when soft to the touch and place on a baking sheet. Place another sheet on top and add some weight to "press" overnight in the refrigerator. The next day, portion cheeks into 2 x 2-in (5 x 5-cm) pieces, ½ in (1 cm) thick (or as close as possible to those dimensions). Season with a little salt and pepper and cook in a non-stick skillet over medium heat, about 4 minutes per side. Deglaze with a little maple syrup and let caramelize.

For the tomatoes:

Lay tomatoes on a cooling rack placed on a cookie sheet. Season cut side of each tomato with an even distribution of all remaining ingredients. Let cure overnight in the refrigerator and cook slowly the next day in an oven at 275°F (135°C), about 30 minutes. Remove and cool to room temperature before serving.

For the banyuls:

Combine all ingredients in a medium-sized saucepan and bring to a simmer. Continue to simmer over low heat until mixture has reached the consistency of corn syrup. Remove and cool to room temperature.

Presentation:

Arrange pieces of pig cheeks on each plate and garnish with tomatoes, shaved radish disks, bocconcini cheese, herbs, olive oil and greens.

Serves 8 as an appetizer, with some pork cheek leftovers

Corn Cob and Aged Cheddar Soufflé

Soufflés, both sweet and savoury, are served every day in bistros all over the world. They have a reputation as being difficult but they are actually a lot of fun to make. Fresh corn for this recipe really makes a difference, but frozen can be used in a pinch. I typically use white Canadian cheddar, but orange cheddar, Gruyère, Gouda or Oka are also great choices. It makes a great side dish for pot roast, roast chicken, roast pork or barbecued chicken.

4 ears fresh corn
½ cup (125 mL) unsalted butter
¾ cup (180 mL) unbleached white flour
2 cups (500 mL) 2% milk
¼ cup (60 mL) minced shallots
1 clove garlic, minced
½ tsp (3 mL) salt
½ tsp (3 mL) ground white pepper
a pinch of freshly grated nutmeg
5 free-range eggs, separated, whites reserved
1 cup (250 mL) grated aged cheddar cheese
2 tbsp (30 mL) butter
3 tbsp (45 mL) grated Parmesan cheese

Remove kernels from corncobs with a sharp knife. Reserve the cobs. Place kernels in a food processor and purée until relatively smooth.

In a small saucepan, melt butter over medium heat and add flour. Mix well until a crumble paste forms. Set aside to cool.

In a second saucepan, combine milk, puréed kernels, corncobs, shallots, garlic, salt, pepper and nutmeg and bring to a boil. Simmer cobs for 30 minutes and remove.

Stirring constantly, add hot liquid to cooled roux in the first saucepan. Simmer on very low heat for 15 minutes. As sauce thickens, stir with a whisk to remove any lumps. Refrigerate until cool.

Beat egg whites to stiff peaks. Add grated cheese and egg yolks to cooled sauce. Grease 6 x 8-oz (250 mL) ramekins with butter and dust with Parmesan. Fill each with mixture and bake in a 425°F (220°C) oven for 10 minutes. Reduce the temperature to 350°F (180°C) and continue cooking for an additional 6 minutes. Serve immediately.

Serves 6

Marinated Passamaquoddy Bay Herring Fillets with Fingerling Potatoes

Chris Aerni, Rossmount Inn, St. Andrews By-the-Sea, New Brunswick

Chris made this dish in 2008 at the inaugural Canadian Chefs' Congress at Eigensinn Farm. He served each of these little pickled herrings on a wooden shingle, giving them a striking and rustic appearance. For many who attended, these delicious chilled seafood appetizers stole the show. The success of this dish depends on the freshness of the herring and its careful handling during filleting. The better the vinegar, the more pleasant the marinated herring is going to be, so don't skimp on the brand. The garnishes can be stuffed into the belly of each fish or served as a side salad.

1 ¼ lb (500 g) fresh herrings (small if possible)
½ cup (125 mL) coarse sea salt
¼ cup (60 mL) minced shallots
¼ cup (60 mL) very finely minced carrots
1 clove garlic, minced
1 whole clove
1 bay leaf
1 sprig fresh thyme
10 whole white peppercorns
2 to 3 cups (500 to 750 mL) white-wine vinegar
6 small fingerling potatoes, cooked and chilled
8 cherry tomatoes
½ cup (125 mL) sour cream
2 tbsp (30 mL) chopped fresh chives

Clean and wash herrings, then remove fillets from the bone with a sharp filleting knife. Lay fillets side by side on a tray. Cover with coarse sea salt for 2 hours, turning every ½ hour. In a bowl, mix all vegetables and spices together. Remove herring from salt, clean and dry with a cloth. In a terrine mould or dish just large enough to fit all the ingredients, stack the fillets with all the mixed aromatics in between the layers. Cover with white wine vinegar and let marinate for 24 hours. Remove stacked fillets from vinegar and discard vegetables.

Slice fingerling potatoes into little coins and each tomato into 3 disks. Mix sour cream and chives together in a small bowl.

Presentation:

Place 1 fillet on a plate, add 3 pieces of potato and a couple of slices of cherry tomato on top and then a teaspoon of chive sour cream. Top off with a second fillet (as if making a sandwich). Serve one or two pieces per person.

Serves 8

General Tao Bacon with Crunchy Cashew Coleslaw

Cooking with bacon is a favourite activity for most Canadian chefs, and pork belly dishes are becoming more and more common. What you are looking for from your butcher is a raw, uncured or smoked pork belly. Once braised, the meat is incredibly tender, and new flavours can be added. Inspired by a dish of General Tao chicken, the sauce below has essences of ginger, sesame and garlic that work unbelievably well when glazed over the succulent pork belly. It is great as an appetizer with the coleslaw, but if served with sticky rice it makes a fine main course as well.

Bacon

1 ½ cups (375 mL) brown sugar
½ cup (125 mL) rock salt
1 tbsp (15 mL) powdered ginger
1 tbsp (15 mL) Chinese five-spice powder
1 pod star anise
1 tbsp (15 mL) cracked peppercorns
½ full pork belly, skin removed (approximately 2 ½ lb or 1 kg)
3 cups (750 mL) beef broth
1 cup (250 mL) sake
1 small onion, coarsely chopped
1 stalk celery, coarsely chopped
3 bay leaves
1 finger of fresh ginger, sliced
2 cloves garlic

Sauce

¼ cup (60 mL) sesame oil
3 tbsp (45 mL) roasted garlic purée (fresh garlic is fine)
½ cup (125 mL) grated ginger
1 tsp (5 mL) Sriracha or Asian hot sauce
1 cup (250 mL) water
1 cup (250 mL) seasoned rice wine vinegar
½ cup (125 mL) mirin (seasoned rice wine)
½ cup (125 mL) sugar
¾ cup (185 mL) liquid honey
¼ cup (60 mL) soy sauce
½ cup (125 mL) oyster sauce
½ cup (125 mL) ketchup
¼ cup (60 mL) cornstarch
¼ cup (60 mL) water

Crunchy Cashew Coleslaw

¼ cup (60 mL) sliced spring onion
2 tbsp (30 mL) sliced pickled ginger
¼ cup (60 mL) crushed toasted cashews
½ cup (125 mL) bean sprouts
½ cup (125 mL) julienned carrot
2 tsp (10 mL) sesame seeds
4 water chestnuts, sliced
½ tsp (3 mL) sesame oil
1 tbsp (15 mL) seasoned rice wine vinegar
salt and pepper to taste

For the bacon:

In a bowl, combine brown sugar, rock salt, powdered ginger, five-spice powder, star anise and cracked peppercorns and mix well. In the bottom of a casserole dish, place ½ of the spice rub and put pork belly on top. Cover belly with remaining spice mix and refrigerate, covered, for 24 hours.

Remove pork belly and brush off spice mixture. Rinse under cold running water and pat dry with paper towels. Place belly in a clean roasting pan or appropriately sized casserole dish.

In a saucepan, heat beef broth, sake, onion, celery, bay leaves, fresh ginger and garlic. As soon as liquid boils remove from the heat and pour over pork belly. Make sure pork is completely submerged in liquid before it goes into the oven. Use a resting rack as a weight if needed.

Cook pork belly overnight in a 175°F (80°C) oven for a minimum of 12 hours. When pork is fork tender remove from the oven and let cool in the liquid. When liquid is cold and congealed remove belly and wipe off any excess braising liquid. Cut pork belly (bacon) into 2 x 2-in (5 x 5-cm) pieces and refrigerate until ready to serve.

At serving time, place 6 pieces of bacon (or 1 piece per person) onto a baking tray lined with parchment paper. Liberally glaze each with cold sauce, using as much as you like, but 2 tbsp (30 mL) per person is about right. Heat bacon in a 350°F (180°C) oven until golden and sticky, or about 15 minutes, with only the top broiler element on.

For the sauce:

Heat all ingredients except cornstarch in a saucepan. Make a slurry with cornstarch and an equal part of water. Whisk into simmering sauce, cool and refrigerate.

For the coleslaw:

In a bowl, simply mix all ingredients together and marinate for 30 minutes before serving.

Presentation:

Place a small mound of coleslaw in the centre of a salad plate and rest glazed bacon on top. Serve immediately.

Serves 12

Crispy Beef Short Ribs

Michael Moffat, Beckta, Ottawa, Ontario

Beef short ribs are a cut of meat prized by almost every chef. The trouble in the restaurant world is getting people to give them a try. Accustomed to neat and tidy *filet mignon* and New York strips, diners often do not know what to do with a short rib on their plate. Do you use a knife and fork, or dig in with your hands like Fred Flintstone? But for flavour there is no more tender and delicious cut of beef. Michael has created a unique appetizer that uses the very best qualities of beef ribs without the complexities and social awkwardness of eating them. This is what I would consider a modern bistro dish, one that uses a lesser cut of meat, cooks it traditionally, but presents it in a slightly unusual way.

4 tbsp (60 mL) canola oil
8 lb (3.5 kg) beef short ribs
2 cups (500 mL) red wine
6 cups (1.5 L) veal stock
½ cup (125 mL) coarsely chopped celery
½ cup (125 mL) chopped carrots
1 cup (250 mL) diced onions
½ bunch thyme
1 bay leaf
10 sheets gelatin
3 eggs
1 cup (250 mL) flour
2 cups (500 mL) crushed corn flakes
3 cups (750 mL) canola oil (second amount)

Heat oil in a large frying pan (the ribs must not be too crowded and the pan must stay very hot during the sear). Caramelize ribs on all sides until deep golden brown in colour. Remove from pan and set aside. Deglaze pan with a little of the wine. Transfer short ribs into an ovenproof pot deep enough to cover them completely with liquid. Add wine, stock, celery, carrots, onions, thyme and bay leaf to pot, adding more stock if necessary to cover. Bring to a boil on the stovetop, then cover and finish in oven at 275°F (135°C) for 2 to 3 hours. The meat should fall off the bone. Cool ribs in the liquid. Pick and shred ribs, removing as much fat as possible. This is easier when meat is cold. Place meat in a shallow casserole dish in a layer about ¾ in (2 cm) thick. Refrigerate until ready for sauce.

For the sauce, strain braising liquid and reduce until thickened slightly and full of flavour. Soak gelatin in cold water until hydrated and add to reduced sauce. Pour sauce over rib meat, making sure meat is just covered. Refrigerate until set into a firm, sliceable terrine. Cut into desired shapes like squares or circles using a cookie cutter or a sharp paring knife. Beat eggs and dredge each piece of sliced terrine in flour, eggs and corn flakes. Dip in eggs and cornflakes a second time. Heat canola oil to 350°F (180°C) (use a deep-fry thermometer to measure the temperature accurately). Deep-fry until crisp, and centre becomes warm and molten.

Serve with a simple crisp salad or some sliced tomatoes.

Serves 8 to 10

Apple, Blue Cheese and Bacon Cheesecake

Michael Howell, Tempest Restaurant, Wolfville, Nova Scotia

This lovely appetizer is great party food for blue cheese lovers. It bakes just like a normal cheesecake and can be served whole or sliced for individual plated portions. When we made this recipe in the test kitchen, we found that, like most cheese, it benefited from sitting out for a while. The cheesecake became spreadable, and all the nutty and smoky flavours of the blue cheese and bacon became more pronounced. Michael serves this with a small salad of baby arugula leaves, fresh apple slices and toast points — classical triangular pieces of toasted sandwich bread.

nonstick vegetable spray

¼ cup (60 mL) freshly grated Parmesan cheese

¼ lb (110 g) Applewood or double-smoked bacon

1 small onion, minced

1 Gala or Gravenstein apple, peeled, cored and cut into medium dice

1 clove garlic, minced

a pinch of sea salt

freshly ground black pepper

12 oz (350 g) cream cheese, at room temperature

1 ½ tbsp (22 mL) wine vinegar

1 ½ tbsp (22 mL) whiskey

5 oz (160 g) locally sourced creamy blue cheese, crumbled

3 eggs

Preheat oven to 275°F (135°C). Spray the inside of a 6-in (15-cm) springform pan with nonstick oil and dust with 2 tablespoons of Parmesan. Set aside.

In a skillet, cook bacon until crisp. Remove excess fat, crumble bacon and reserve. Discard all but 2 tbsp (30 mL) of bacon fat. Add onion to fat in the pan and cook over medium heat until soft, about 2 minutes. Add apple and garlic and continue cooking until onion is very tender and apple has lost its raw look (5 to 6 more minutes). Remove from heat, season with salt and pepper and set aside to cool.

In a mixer with a paddle attachment, beat cream cheese until soft. Add vinegar, whiskey, blue cheese, remaining Parmesan and eggs (one egg at a time). Add bacon and apple reserves. Mix well. Pour batter into the prepared pan, place on top of a cookie sheet and place in the oven. Cook for 2 to 2 ½ hours. Check the cake after 2 hours. Insert a clean, dry knife into cake — it should come out clean. The top should have barely coloured, and the surface will be flawless. Remove to a rack and cool in the pan for 1 hour.

Cover with cling film and refrigerate until well set. To serve, cut with a long, sharp knife dipped in warm water to prevent sticking. Serve with crisp toasts, freshly sliced apples, and arugula salad.

Serves 12

Hare Ragout with Seville Orange and Rosemary Gnocchi

Charles Part, Restaurant Les Fougères, Chelsea, Quebec

Cooking with rabbit and hare is a tradition in Quebec and many parts of eastern Canada, especially in winter when they are trapped or snared. Rabbit fricassee, stew with dumplings or biscuit-crusted pie (not to be confused with *rappie* pie, a different Acadian dish altogether) fill French Canadian kitchens all winter long and have done for centuries. "We source our hare from trappers in La Petite-Nation region east of Chelsea," adds Chef Part. "The meat is darker and more flavourful than rabbit. The Seville orange and rosemary accents in the tender gnocchi bring welcome citrus and herbal notes to the rich ragout."

Hare Ragout

½ cup (125 mL) olive oil
2 tbsp (30 mL) butter
6 oz (180 g) lardon bacon, diced
1 hare, jointed, approximately 3 lb (1.5 kg)
1 tsp (5 mL) sea salt
1 tsp (5 mL) freshly ground black pepper
1 large cooking onion, finely chopped
1 large carrot, finely chopped
6 whole garlic cloves, peeled
2 tbsp (30 mL) tomato paste
4 chopped tomatoes
2 tbsp (30 mL) red currant jelly
¼ cup (60 mL) balsamic vinegar
½ bottle (375 mL) dry white wine
2 tbsp (30 mL) crushed juniper berries
leaves from 2 sprigs of fresh thyme
3 bay leaves

Seville Orange and Rosemary Gnocchi

3 large Yukon gold potatoes
3 egg yolks
1 tbsp (15 mL) fresh chopped rosemary
2 tbsp (30 mL) Seville orange marmalade
zest from 1 lemon
zest from 1 orange
1 ¼ cup (310 mL) flour
2 tbsp (30 mL) butter
1 cup grated Gré des Champs or Parmigiano Reggiano
   (to serve)

For the ragout:

In a heavy-bottomed, ovenproof casserole dish, heat olive oil, butter and bacon over medium-high heat until fat is rendered from bacon.

Add hare pieces to the casserole and brown well on all sides. Season hare with salt and pepper. Add onion, carrot and garlic and continue to cook, stirring occasionally, until vegetables have started to brown. Add tomato paste, tomatoes, red currant jelly, balsamic vinegar, white wine, juniper berries, thyme and bay leaves.

Cover with a lid and cook in an oven at 375°F (190°C) for 1 hour, or until hare is tender. The bones can be removed if desired and the meat roughly pulled apart using two forks.

For the gnocchi:

Bake potatoes in their skins at 350°F (180°C) for about 1 hour, or until flesh is soft inside. Let rest until cool enough to handle, then spoon out flesh and pass it through a ricer or food mill. Mound milled potato onto a floured board. Make a well in the centre and add egg yolks, rosemary, marmalade and citrus zests, reserving a little rosemary and orange zest for garnish. Using a fork, stir all ingredients in the well together, incorporating potato bit by bit. Gradually add just enough flour to form a tender dough and knead gently and briefly to form a ball.

Divide dough into quarters. Roll each quarter into a ¼-in (5-mm) diameter rope and cut into pieces on the diagonal. Throw into boiling salted water. As soon as gnocchi rise to the top, strain and toss with butter.

To serve, spoon gnochi into serving bowls along with a ladle of hare ragout, grated Gré des Champs or Parmigiano Reggiano and a garnish of fresh rosemary and orange zest.

Serves 6

Foie Gras Poutine

Steve Vardy, Black Cat Bistro, Ottawa, Ontario

What would a Canadian bistro cookbook be without a poutine recipe? Over the past few years chefs have had a lot of fun with different versions of this late-night sidewalk snack. People who love it are passionate about their poutine. Steve first served me his Foie Gras Poutine on my cross-Canada adventure in 2004. It was pure bliss. I may have wanted to "borrow" this dish from Steve for my own restaurant but I avoided the temptation out of respect for his creation. When the recipe testers for this book and I made this, we simply could not fault it in any way. We served it with a *Greco di Tuffo* from Italy and the whole experience was perfect.

Foie Gras Sauce
1 cup (250 mL) red wine
¼ cup (60 mL) sliced shallots
⅓ cup (85 mL) diced carrots
5 sprigs Italian parsley
4 sprigs fresh thyme
1 bay leaf
2 cloves garlic, sliced
6 black peppercorns
2 cups (500 mL) veal stock
5 oz (150 g) foie gras
salt and pepper to taste

Poutine
6 cups (1.5 L) peanut or canola oil (for deep frying)
4 large russet or yellow-fleshed potatoes (cut into French fries)
1 tsp (5 mL) fleur de sel or coarse sea salt
4 slices foie gras, 3 oz (90 g) each, cut 1 in (2.5 cm) thick
12 oz (325 g) cheese curds, at room temperature
2 tbsp (30 mL) chopped chives (for garnish)
a few grindings of fresh black pepper

For the foie gras sauce:

In a medium saucepan, bring wine, shallots, carrots, parsley, thyme, bay leaf, garlic and peppercorns to a simmer and reduce until almost all of the liquid has evaporated. Add veal stock and simmer until reduced by one-quarter, or until it reaches sauce consistency. Strain sauce, return to saucepan and bring to a boil. Pour hot sauce into a blender and purée with foie gras. Adjust seasoning with salt and pepper. The sauce cannot be boiled after this point, just kept warm, otherwise the emulsion will break.

For the poutine:

Using a steep-sided, heavy-bottomed saucepan, heat oil to 275°F (135°C), monitoring the temperature with a deep-fry thermometer. "Blanch" fries in oil for about 3 minutes (the fries should not take on any colour during this process) and rest them on a plate lined with clean paper towels. Allow to cool to room temperature. The fries will likely need to be cooked in 2 small batches.

Increase the heat until oil temperature reaches 350°F (180°C). Fry the fries a second time, until golden brown. Remove from oil and season with sea salt.

Heat a cast iron pan until very hot. Sear foie gras in the pan for about 1 minute per side, depending on the thickness. They should be golden brown but not overcooked (slightly underdone or cool in the middle is perfect).

To serve, mound French fries in the centre of a pasta or shallow soup bowl. Sprinkle liberally with cheese curds and place a piece of foie gras on top. Drizzle warm foie gras sauce over everything and garnish with a grinding of fresh black pepper and some chopped chives. Serve immediately as the fries will become soggy if allowed to sit.

Serves 4

Pan-roasted Sweetbreads with Parsnip Purée, Spring Spinach and Veal Jus

Martín Ruiz Salvador, Fleur de Sel, Lunenburg, Nova Scotia

Martin brings together traditional French cooking and local ingredients better than anyone I know. The first time I dined at Fleur de Sel I was intrigued by the familiarity of the flavours: dishes like bouillabaisse, smoked salmon traditionally garnished with egg and crème fraîche and foie gras with brioche and apple compote. The dish Martin presents here is my personal favourite and is yet another example of how offal meats are creatively used now in Canada's finest restaurants as well as in the best bistros of Europe. The veal jus really makes this dish decadent, so if you feel you can't make it from scratch try to purchase pre-made frozen veal jus from a high-end deli or butcher if possible.

Parsnips and Spinach

1 lb (450 g) peeled parsnips, diced into ¼-in (5-mm) cubes
3 large shallots, finely chopped
4 tbsp (60 mL) butter
2 cups (500 mL) 35% cream
1 tsp (5 mL) sea salt
freshly ground pepper to taste
4 bunches organic spinach (about 8 oz / 225g)

Sweetbreads

1 lb (450 g) fresh veal sweetbreads
⅓ cup (85 mL) veal jus reduction (recipe follows)
freshly ground black pepper
2 tsp (10 mL) canola oil
1 tbsp (30 mL) butter
1 tsp (5 mL) fleur de sel or good flaky sea salt

Veal Jus

5 lb (2.25 kg) veal bones
5 lb (2.25 kg) veal shank or beef shank with meat
2 lb (900 g) coarsely chopped onion
1 lb (450 g) coarsely chopped celery
1 lb (450 g) coarsely chopped carrot
½ lb (225 g) white of leek, optional
2 tbsp (30 mL) canola oil
1 large ripe tomato, coarsely chopped
2 cloves garlic
4 bay leaves
4 sprigs fresh thyme (or 2 tsp dried thyme)
½ bunch Italian parsley
2 tbsp (30 mL) whole black peppercorns
2 cups (500 mL) sherry
8 cups (2 litres) unsalted beef stock
salt and pepper to taste

For the parsnips and spinach:

Sweat parsnips and half the minced shallots in 2 tablespoons of the butter. When the parsnips are beginning to become soft add the cream, bring to a boil and reduce by one-third (this should take about 15 minutes). Blend the parsnips and cream in a food processor or blender until smooth. Season to taste with salt and pepper. Set purée aside; reheat just before serving in a saucepan or even the microwave.

Bring a pot of well-salted water to a boil (use 1 tablespoon of salt for every gallon of water). Clean the spinach by removing any thick or woody stems and rinse the leaves under cold water in case there is dirt or sand present. Blanch the 4 bunches of spinach in salted water for just 20 seconds and remove immediately from the boiling water. Plunge the spinach into an ice-water bath to shock quickly, then remove from the ice water and drain well in a colander.

When you are ready to serve the meal, reheat the spinach in a sauté pan. Simply sweat the remaining quantity of minced shallots in the remaining 2 tablespoons of butter. Add the wilted spinach to the pan and cook for about 2 minutes over medium heat. Season with sea salt and pepper to taste.

For the sweetbread:

Preheat oven to 375° F.

Remove all loose membrane and any discolored spots from the veal sweetbreads, using your fingers or a small paring knife. Season the sweetbreads with some freshly ground black pepper. In a frying pan add canola oil, bring to medium heat, and add the sweetbreads. Sear on one side for one minute, add the butter, flip them, and place in the preheated oven for 15 minutes. Let rest for 5 minutes prior to serving.

For the veal jus:

Roast the veal bones and shanks in a 400° F (200° C) oven for 30 minutes or until golden brown. As the bones are roasting begin caramelizing the onions, celery, carrot, and leek in the canola oil. When the vegetables are brown add the tomato and garlic and cook for an additional 10 minutes.

Remove the bones from the oven and add to the pot of vegetables. Add the herbs, peppercorns, and sherry to the pot and bring to a boil. Reduce the sherry by half. Add the stock and top up with water if necessary. Simmer for a minimum of 8 hours (overnight is better). Strain the broth into a smaller saucepan. Reduce the veal jus until it coats the back of a spoon. Season with salt and pepper if desired.

Yields 1 cup (250 mL)

Presentation:

Reheat parsnip purée and spinach as directed above. Put a dollop of purée in the center of a dinner plate. Place the spinach to the side of the purée. Remove sweetbreads from oven and place next to spinach. Drizzle veal jus on top of sweetbreads, garnish with fleur de sel and enjoy.

Serves 6

Pickled Bison Tenderloin with Dijon Cherry Vinaigrette and Mustard Greens

Rémi Cousyn, Calories Restaurant, Saskatoon, Saskatchewan

Beef carpaccio is a lovely summer treat, but there is no reason why it can't be enjoyed in the cold winter weather, too. Carpaccio is nothing more than tenderloin that has been seasoned, often seared and thinly sliced. Here Rémi Cousyn has pickled a bison tenderloin with many great flavours and skipped the searing, allowing the marinade to "cook" the outer layer of the tender meat. It can be sliced like a carpaccio, laid out on a plate and garnished with beautiful spicy mustard greens and a cherry vinaigrette. Rémi uses dried carmine jewel cherries, but whatever type you can find will work well, as long as they are sweet.

Pickled Bison Tenderloin

1 tbsp (15 mL) fresh thyme leaves
2 tbsp (30 mL) fresh parsley
1 tbsp (15 mL) fresh rosemary
2 tsp (10 mL) white pepper
1 tbsp (15 mL) black pepper
1 tsp (5 mL) green pepper
½ tsp (3 mL) Szechuan pepper
1 tsp (5 mL) juniper berries
½ tsp (3 mL) cloves
1 tsp (5 mL) fresh Thai chili pepper, seeds removed
1 tbsp (15 mL) sugar
⅔ cup (180 mL) coarse salt
2 tbsp (30 mL) grappa
3 lb (1.3 kg) bison tenderloin (beef is a good substitute)

Dijon Cherry Vinaigrette

½ cup (125 mL) sweet dried carmine jewel cherries, finely chopped
1 tbsp (15 mL) Dijon mustard
3 tbsp (45 mL) cherry juice reduction
3 tbsp (45 mL) red wine vinegar
1 tbsp (15 mL) reserved spices
½ cup (125 mL) olive and canola oil blend

Salad Garnishes

2 cups (500 mL) baby mustard greens
4 oz (125 g) shaved Parmesan cheese (optional)

For the tenderloin:

Prepare all herbs and spices by chopping or cracking finely. Mix together all ingredients except tenderloin. Dry bison tenderloin with a paper towel, rub with spice mixture and wrap individual loins in plastic wrap. Refrigerate for 3 days.

Unwrap meat and scrape off excess spices, reserving a small amount for the Dijon Cherry Vinaigrette. Rinse well under running water to remove all spices. Slice tenderloin thinly, allowing about 6 slices per person. To slice tenderloin, wrap it tightly in plastic wrap or foil and freeze until flesh is just firm, not frozen through.

For the vinaigrette:

Mix all ingredients together in a bowl until blended.

Presentation:

Lay 6 slices of tenderloin per person in a single layer over a large plate. Dress top of bison with 2 tbsp (30 mL) cherry dressing and a handful of mustard greens. Sprinkle with some Parmesan cheese shavings and a grinding of fresh black pepper if desired.

Serves 8

Foie Gras Crème Brûlée with Black Pepper Cherry Biscotti

Michael Dekker, Rouge, Calgary, Alberta

Michael Dekker is responsible for the kitchens at Rouge in Calgary every day. The cuisine is progressive and challenging but rooted in very honest and traditional recipes. In this unique appetizer Michael combines two of the richest and most luxurious bistro dishes on earth into one: crème brûlée and succulent foie gras. Serve this with a Sauternes or sweeter Muscat for a once-in-a-lifetime first course.

Crème Brûlée

1 cup (250 mL) 35% cream
1 tsp (5 mL) sugar
4 oz (125 g) foie gras, in ½-in (1-cm) cubes
3 egg yolks
½ tsp (3 mL) sea salt
¼ tsp (1 mL) freshly ground black pepper
2 tbsp (30 mL) sugar (for brûlée tops)

Black Pepper and Cherry Biscotti

1 cup (250 mL) all-purpose flour
2 tbsp (30 mL) sugar
¼ tsp (1 mL) baking powder
1 tsp (5 mL) fresh cracked black pepper
¼ tsp (1 mL) salt
2 tbsp (30 mL) cold butter (no substitutes)
1 egg
1 tbsp (15 mL) milk
½ cup (125 mL) halved candied cherries

For the brûlée:

Combine cream and sugar in a saucepan and bring mixture to the scalding point. Remove from heat and add foie gras. Place mixture in blender and blend on high until smooth. In a separate bowl, whisk egg yolks until smooth. Temper cream and foie gras mixture into egg yolks by adding a small ladle at a time, whisking continuously. Season with salt and pepper. Strain mixture through a sieve or fine-meshed chinois.

   Pour mixture into small (3-oz / 90-g) ramekins and place them in a roasting pan or casserole dish. Pour hot water into the roasting pan until it comes halfway up the sides of the ramekins. Cook at 300°F (150°C) for 20 to 30 minutes until just set. Refrigerate for at least 6 hours before serving. Sprinkle tops with raw sugar and heat with a propane or butane torch until dark golden brown. Serve with Black Pepper and Cherry Biscotti.

Yields 6 small brûlées

For the biscotti:

In a bowl, combine flour, sugar, baking powder, black pepper and salt. Cut butter into the mixture until it resembles coarse crumbs. In another bowl, beat egg and milk until blended, then stir into dry ingredients until blended. Stir in cherries (the dough will be crumbly). Divide dough in half, and shape each half into a ball. On an ungreased baking sheet, roll each ball into a 10 x 2 ½-in (25 x 6-cm) rectangle. Bake at 350°F (180°C) for 30 to 35 minutes, or until golden brown. Carefully remove to wire racks and cool for 20 minutes. Transfer to a cutting board and cut diagonally with a sharp knife into ¼-in (5-mm) slices. Place cut side down on ungreased baking sheets. Bake for 5 minutes or until firm. Remove to wire racks to cool and store in an airtight container.

Yields 6 to 8 biscotti

Charcuterie Board with Red Onion Jam

Steve Mitton, Murray Street, Ottawa, Ontario

During the preparations for this book I was taken to a new Ottawa restaurant called Murray Street. I tagged along expecting very little and was happy to find a chef's dream: high-quality charcuterie dishes, house-made in the traditional style. This way of cooking is a bit of a lost art in North America, although making pâtés, terrines and sausages goes back centuries in many cultures, especially in France and Quebec. A traditional bistro would always have cold meats on hand to feed the common man. I am thrilled to see the demand for charcuterie rising in cities and hope these dishes remain in our Canadian bistro food culture.

Country Terrine of Pork

2 shallots, minced

1 tbsp (15 mL) butter

2 ½ tsp (13 mL) dried herbes de Provence

2 oz (60 mL) cognac or brandy

2 ½ lb (1.2 kg) ground pork

½ lb (225 g) smoked bacon, finely chopped

4 cloves garlic, very finely chopped

2 ½ tsp (13 mL) salt

1 ½ tsp (8 mL) ground allspice

1 tsp (5 mL) white pepper

2 eggs, beaten

⅓ cup (85 mL) 35% cream

14 slices smoked bacon (for wrapping terrine)

1 smoked pork tenderloin, whole

Duck Liver Mousse

2.2 lb (1 kg) fresh duck livers

3 tbsp (45 mL) butter

2 tbsp (30 mL) sherry

2 tbsp (30 mL) local honey

1 tsp (5 mL) white truffle oil

1 tsp (5 mL) salt

1 cup (250 mL) cold butter (second amount), cubed

3 tbsp (45 mL) 35% cream

½ cup (125 mL) melted duck fat

Murray Street Cretons

2 lb (900 g) ground pork

1 lb (450 g) duck fat

2 tsp (10 mL) ground cloves

2 cups (500 mL) dry white wine

2 tbsp (30 mL) salt (or to taste)

4 cloves garlic, very finely minced

4 shallots, minced

½ cup (125 mL) fine breadcrumbs

Red Onion Jam

1 cup (250 mL) cranberry juice

½ cup (125 mL) chokecherry or Saskatoon berry vinegar

1 cup (250 mL) white sugar

12 red onions, diced

For the terrine:

Sauté shallots in butter with herbes de Provence for 3 minutes and deglaze with cognac or brandy. Remove from heat and add to a large mixing bowl with all the other ingredients except the tenderloin and bacon strips. Mix well. Line a terrine mould with bacon slices and fill halfway with ground pork mixture. Place tenderloin on top, centred in the mould. Fill the terrine with remaining pork mixture and pat down. Fold over bacon strips to completely wrap filling. Place mould in a roasting pan or larger casserole dish and fill pan halfway up the sides with hot water to make a bain-marie. Cook uncovered at 375°F (190°C) until the internal temperature reads more than 145°F (63°C). Refrigerate until well chilled and cut into ½-in (1 cm) slices to serve.

Serves 12 to 14

For the mousse:

Cook duck livers to medium (about 4 to 5 minutes) in first amount of butter and deglaze the pan with sherry. Cool livers and blend in a food processor with honey, truffle oil and salt to taste.

Continue to blend, and add second amount of butter in small cubes through the hatch at the top of the food processor, keeping mixture as cold as possible to prevent separating. Add cream slowly until smooth then spoon mousse into ramekins or small lion's-head bowls. Use a spoon to flatten tops evenly and gently spoon some warm duck fat over the tops to form an airtight seal. Refrigerate immediately. Serve chilled with crisp Melba toast or French bread.

Yields 3 cups, or 12 small ramekins

For the cretons:

Place all ingredients except breadcrumbs in a heavy-bottomed stainless steel pot. Cook slowly over low heat, stirring occasionally, for about 45 minutes. Add breadcrumbs and cook a further 5 minutes. Season again and pour into containers, jars or terrine moulds. Top with a ¼-in (5-mm) layer of duck fat if you wish to keep the cretons for a while in the refrigerator. Serve with homemade pickles and mustard.

Yields 4 cups (1 L)

For the jam:

Bring liquids and sugar to a simmer and reduce by half. Add onions and cook over low heat until onions are translucent and jam has thickened. Cool and serve alongside pâtés, terrines and cold meats.

Yields 6 cups, or 3 x 500 mL Mason jars

Chives' Party Chips 'n' Dips: Chermula Spiced Feta, Caramelized Onion and Chèvre, Baked Brie with Brown Sugar and Spiced Pita Crisps

At one point in every year there is cause to make something for a party, either yours or someone else's. In the restaurant world, we chefs may try to cook food that is hyper-creative and inspiring for our guests, but even *we* host functions and receptions where simple party dips are warranted. These are three that I have turned to. They showcase Canadian cheeses, which are available year-round and are always delicious. Simple pita crisps make a great accompaniment as they are low in saturated fat and pita bread is baked in small independent bakeries all over Canada.

Chermula Spiced Feta Dip

2 small red onions

3 tbsp (45 mL) extra-virgin olive oil

1 tsp (5 mL) cumin

1 tsp (5 mL) paprika

1 tsp (5 mL) fennel seed

1 tsp (5 mL) chili flakes

1 tsp (5 mL) turmeric

juice of 1 lemon

2 cups (500 mL) feta cheese

¼ to ½ cup (60 to 125 mL) extra-virgin olive oil
   (second amount)

Caramelized Onion and Goat Cheese Dip

5 cups (1.25 L) sliced white onions

2 tbsp (30 mL) olive oil

2 tbsp (30 mL) butter

¼ cup (60 mL) sherry or white wine

1 ½ cups (375 mL) fresh creamy goat's cheese, at room
   temperature

1 cup (250 mL) cream cheese, at room temperature

2 tbsp (30 mL) roasted garlic purée

1 tsp (5 mL) hot sauce (like Tabasco)

1 tsp (5 mL) Worcestershire sauce

salt and pepper to taste

2 tbsp (30 mL) chopped chives (for garnish)

Baked Brie with Brown Sugar and Pecans

2 sheets all-butter puff pastry (8 x 10 in/20 x 25 cm)

1 medium-sized wheel Quebec brie (6-in/15-cm diameter)

2 tbsp (30 mL) softened butter

½ cup (125 mL) brown sugar

½ cup (125 mL) toasted pecans, chopped or whole

1 egg, beaten

aged balsamic vinegar (to drizzle over top)

Spiced Pita Crisps

6 large fresh pita breads (10-in/25-cm diameter), or 10 small (6-in/5-cm diameter)

½ cup (125 mL) extra-virgin olive oil

1 tsp (5 mL) dried basil

1 tsp (5 mL) dried oregano

2 tsp (10 mL) paprika

½ tsp (3 mL) freshly cracked black pepper

⅛ tsp (0.5 mL) cayenne pepper

1 tsp (5 mL) fleur de sel (or other flaky sea salt)

For the feta dip:

Coarsely chop red onions and sauté in olive oil until they are soft and have no colour. In a separate pan, combine cumin, paprika, fennel seed, chili flakes and turmeric. Toast spices until they just begin to smoke and smell fragrant, then transfer to a coffee mill and grind to a fine powder. Add spice mixture to onions and transfer to a food processor. With the motor running add lemon juice and feta cheese. If needed, you may add the remaining extra-virgin olive oil to adjust the texture of the dip.

Yields 3 cups (750 mL)

For the onion and cheese dip:

Caramelize onions in oil and butter over medium heat until deep brown and sweet. This will take about an hour. Add sherry to deglaze, and reduce until all the liquid has gone.

In a food processor cream together the cheeses, garlic, seasoning sauces, salt and pepper. Pour dip into a mixing bowl and fold in the caramelized onions. (Do not purée onions with cheese as they add a nice texture.)

Chill for one hour before serving and garnish with chives.

Yields 3 ½ cups (875 mL)

For the baked brie dip:

Preheat oven to 425°F (220°C). Place one sheet of chilled, but fully thawed, puff pastry on a parchment-lined baking tray. Place brie in the centre and spread butter evenly on top of cheese rind. Cover with sugar and sprinkle with pecans. Brush a little egg along bottom edges of second piece of puff pastry and set on top. Using a pastry cutter or pizza cutter, cut away some of the excess, but leave enough so that you can form a seal between the top and bottom layer. Curl pastry upwards with your fingertips (this will help prevent seepage of molten cheese and sugar). Brush top again with eggwash and bake in the oven until dark golden brown, about 30 minutes. Allow pastry to become quite crisp and firm, as puff pastry often looks brown and fully cooked when it isn't.

Remove from the oven and place on a large round serving tray. Rest for 5 minutes before serving as the cheese will be extremely hot and may burn mouths. Drizzle some very good aged balsamic vinegar over the top of each serving if desired.

Serves 8 to 10

For the pita crisps:

Preheat oven to 300°F (150°C). Trim away sides of pita bread, making a large square. Slice into rectangular pieces about 2 x 4 in (5 x10 cm) and peel top and bottom pieces apart so you have thin pieces of bread. You should have about 6 to 8 pieces per full piece of bread.

In a mixing bowl combine oil and all the spices except salt and whisk together. Add bread slices to the oil and gently fold them over and over to coat them. Lay each piece out onto a baking tray in a single layer. Sprinkle evenly with a little sea salt. If pitas look a bit dry, drizzle a little extra oil over the top. Bake in oven until slightly browned and quite crisp, about 10 to 12 minutes.

Yields enough chips for one of the above dips (or 8 to 10 people as a snack)

Oyster and Snow Crab Gratin

This is a fun way to cook with oysters, and the presentation is beautiful. Three of these beautiful appetizers is all anyone needs as they are rich. In Nova Scotia, particularly in Cape Breton, snow (or queen) crab is available year round, as are oysters. There may be a lull in the local oyster supplies where the water freezes over, such as here in Nova Scotia. We get ours near Big Island, but P.E.I. Malpeque and Pacific oysters from B.C. are incredible.

1 large snow crab
18 large choice oysters
2 tbsp (30 mL) butter
¼ cup (60 mL) minced red onions or shallots
½ cup (125 mL) sour cream
½ cup (125 mL) softened cream cheese
juice and zest of 1 lemon
1 tsp (5 mL) grated horseradish
1 tsp (5 mL) Worcestershire sauce
1 tsp (5 mL) hot sauce such as Tabasco
¼ tsp (1 mL) salt
¼ tsp (1 mL) pepper
2 tbsp (30 mL) chopped chives
½ cup (125 mL) panko-style or fresh breadcrumbs
2 tbsp (30 mL) melted butter

Cook snow crab legs in 1 in (2.5 cm) of water for 10 minutes, or steam them for the same period in a double boiler. Cool and remove meat from shells. Make sure meat contains no bits of shell or cartilage, and pick into ½-in (1-cm) chunks. One large crab should deliver about 1 cup (250 mL) of cooked meat.

Shuck oysters using a proper oyster knife, and detach meat from adductor muscle underneath. Pour off oyster liquor into a small, fine sieve to remove any sand or bits of shell, and reserve. Take bottom half of each oyster shell (the side with the deeper bowl shape) and rinse very well under running water. It is a good idea to scrub shells with a brush as well to remove any sand. Dry shells and place a single oyster in each. Refrigerate until ready for the oven.

Sauté onions or shallots in butter until translucent. Add to a food processor along with sour cream, cream cheese, lemon, horseradish, Worcestershire, Tabasco, seasonings and reserved oyster liquor. Purée until smooth. Remove the processor from its base and add picked crabmeat and chopped chives. Fold gently together so crab does not break apart too much.

Combine breadcrumbs and melted butter in a small bowl.

To assemble gratins, divide crab mixture amongst the oysters in their shells. Spread evenly and sprinkle with breadcrumbs. Broil gratins in a preheated 500°F (260°C) oven until breadcrumbs are golden and cheese is bubbling. Allow to stand for 3 minutes before serving.

Serves 6

Panisse with Roasted Teardrop Tomatoes and Olive Tapenade

Renee Lavallée, Five Fishermen, Halifax, Nova Scotia

Panisse is a simple chickpea-flour bread that is fried until crispy. The dish originates from the area around Nice in France. Renee has paired it with wonderful little tomatoes that you can find from greenhouse growers year-round. Roasting brings out the sweetness that is sometimes lacking in off-season tomatoes. This is a summery dish that can be enjoyed during colder weather as a vegetarian appetizer or with a piece of roasted fish like halibut or cod.

Panisse

3 cups (750 mL) water
¼ cup (60 mL) extra-virgin olive oil
2 tsp (10 mL) salt
1 ½ cups (375 mL) chickpea flour
2 tbsp (30 mL) finely sliced (chiffonade) fresh basil
¼ tsp (1 mL) freshly ground black pepper
¼ cup (60 mL) olive oil (for pan frying)

Roasted Teardrop Tomatoes

2 cups (500 mL) red and yellow teardrop tomatoes
3 tbsp (45 mL) extra-virgin olive oil
several sprigs thyme
2 cloves garlic, peeled and sliced
¼ tsp (1 mL) salt
¼ tsp (1 mL) pepper

Tapenade

1 cup (250 mL) pitted Kalamata olives
1 anchovy fillet
1 clove garlic
zest of 1 lemon
¼ to ⅓ cup (60 to 85 mL) extra-virgin olive oil
salt and pepper to taste

For the panisse:

Bring water, oil and salt to a low boil. Whisk in chickpea flour, being careful to prevent lumps. Stir with a wooden spoon, about 10 minutes, until it has a thick consistency, similar to porridge. Add basil and adjust seasonings.

Pour panisse mixture onto a greased baking sheet to a thickness of about ½ in (1 cm) and refrigerate for 2 hours. Cut into desired shapes, such as circles, triangles or rectangular strips. Preheat a nonstick or well-seasoned cast iron pan on high, add olive oil and fry panisse on both sides, until golden brown. Thicker panisse portions may need to bake for 5 or 7 minutes in a 350°F (180°C) oven to finish cooking.

Place a hot piece of panisse in the centre of each plate and top with a liberal amount of tapenade (about 2 tbsp/30 mL or so). Add 3 or 4 tomatoes on top and garnish with a few leaves of thyme if desired.

Serves 8, with leftovers

For the roasted tomatoes:

Preheat oven to 400°F (200°C) and place tomatoes on a baking tray. Drizzle generously with olive oil, thyme sprigs, garlic, salt and pepper. Mix everything together with your hands (they're your best tool for this job) and roast for 10 to 15 minutes, or until the tomatoes are splitting on their sides. Remove from oven and set aside, but make sure to keep cooled tomatoes in their roasting liquids.

For the tapenade:

In a food processor, mix olives, anchovy, garlic and lemon zest together with a little olive oil. Start to purée while adding a slow stream of olive oil. This should be a fairly loose tapenade, so don't worry about adding too much oil. Check for seasonings, and set aside.

Yields 1 ½ cups (325 mL)

Brown Sugar Glazed Smoked Salmon with Buckwheat Blinis, Crème Fraîche and Sturgeon Caviar

Derek Mayes, Markham Resorts, Toronto, Ontario

Smoked salmon has become recognized as a great Canadian product. This recipe is basically a hot-smoked version that you can prepare over your barbecue or a household smoker (as suggested). I like this method as the planks mentioned are available at nearly every grocery store year-round. If you have a cold smoker, follow the procedure for cold smoking using shaved wood chips. Salmon, unfortunately, has received much bad press in recent years, some of it deserved. But there are more and more sustainable aquaculture farms popping up and the industry is responding to "greener" demands in our food systems. Farmed salmon is a complex issue and one that requires attention from all consumers.

Salmon

8 cups (2 L) water
½ cup (125 mL) kosher or pickling salt
½ cup (125 mL) white sugar
½ cup (125 mL) brown sugar
juice and zest of 2 lemons
2 tsp (10 mL) cracked black peppercorns
½ bunch fresh parsley
2 bay leaves
2 cloves garlic, crushed
1 orange, sliced
1 lime, sliced
1 small onion, sliced
1 x 3-lb (1.5-kg) side of fresh salmon, skin on, pin bones removed
1 large plank alder wood (apple or maple works as well)
freshly ground black pepper
¼ cup (60 mL) packed brown sugar
2 tbsp (30 mL) water

Buckwheat Blinis

2 cups (500 mL) warm milk (at 110°F/45°C)
1 envelope active dry yeast
1 tsp (5 mL) sugar
1 cup (250 mL) buckwheat flour
4 eggs, beaten
¼ cup (60 mL) sour cream
½ cup (125 mL) 35% cream
½ tsp (3 mL) salt
1 ⅓ cups (335 mL) all-purpose flour
cooking spray

Garnish

¾ cup (185 mL) crème fraîche
2 tbsp (30 mL) chopped fresh chives
1 x 2-oz (60-g) jar sturgeon caviar (from New Brunswick) or salmon roe
fresh chive batons

To marinate the salmon:

Pour water into a large bowl or small bucket. If you must use a pot, use one that does not contain aluminum. Stir in kosher salt, white sugar, brown sugar, lemon juice and zest, pepper, parsley and bay leaves. Add garlic, orange, lime and onion. Soak salmon in this brine for 12 to 36 hours.

To smoke and glaze the salmon:

Submerge wood plank in water, placing a heavy object on top of it to prevent floating. Soak for 2 hours if possible. Preheat an outdoor smoker at 160 to 180°F (70 to 80°C). Remove salmon from brine and rinse thoroughly under cold running water, then pat dry with paper towels. Remove plank from water, and lay fish on plank. Season with black pepper. Smoke salmon for at least 2 hours, checking after 1 ½ hours for doneness. The fish is done when it flakes with a fork, but it should not be too salty. As the fish smokes, the salt content reduces. Adjust the cooking time and saltiness to your taste. Smoking a fillet can take 2 to 6 hours depending on your taste, the size of the fillet, and the fat content of the fish.

During the last 30 minutes of smoking, mix brown sugar and water together to form a paste. Brush liberally onto salmon.

For the blinis:

Pour warm milk into a large bowl, then sprinkle with yeast and let soften (dissolve) for 5 minutes. Stir in sugar and buckwheat flour, cover and let rise for 1 hour. Stir in eggs, sour cream, 35% cream, salt and all-purpose flour until a batter forms. Cover again, and let rise for 2 hours. Heat a large skillet over medium heat. Spray with cooking spray, then pour in small amounts of batter to form 1 ½-in (4-cm) blinis. Cook until blinis begin to set and dry, and the bubbles begin to burst, about 2 minutes. Flip over and continue cooking until browned on the other side, about 1 minute.

Mix crème fraîche and chopped chives together in a small mixing bowl until smooth.

Presentation:

Place 2 blinis overlapping on a plate. Carve or flake approximately 4 to 5 oz (120 to 150 g) of salmon on top. Top with a tablespoon of chive crème fraîche and a teaspoon of sturgeon caviar. Lay 2 chive batons against the salmon.

Serves 6, with leftover salmon

Bison Hump and Saskatoon Berry Perogies

Scott Pohorelic, River Café, Calgary, Alberta

Scott's perogies are well-known and definitely have a place in Western Canadian food culture. Polish immigrants brought these popular treats to us and many chefs have used their culinary license to make new fillings. Potato and cheese is probably the most common, served with sour cream, fried onions and sometimes bacon. The addition of wild Saskatoon berries in Scott's braised-bison filling is a lovely sweet and tangy element in an otherwise rich and filling dish. If you can't find bison, try beef, pork or venison butt roasts.

Perogy Filling

4 lb (2 kg) bison hump (or chuck), cut into 3-in (7.5-cm) thick steaks
1 tsp (5 mL) salt
1 tsp (5 mL) pepper
3 cups (750 mL) bison or beef stock
½ cup (125 mL) red wine or sherry
1 small onion, coarsely chopped
1 celery stalk, coarsely chopped
1 medium carrot, coarsely chopped
1 garlic clove, smashed
2 tbsp (30 mL) sherry vinegar
1 bay leaf
1 tsp (5 mL) whole peppercorns
10 juniper berries
1 sprig fresh rosemary (or a pinch of dried)
1 sprig fresh thyme (or a pinch of dried)
2 cups (500 mL) Saskatoon berries
1 cup (250 mL) Caramelized Onions (recipe follows)
salt and pepper to taste
4 tbsp (60 mL) butter (for frying cooked perogies)

Dough

2 ⅓ cups (585 mL) flour (plus extra for kneading)
1 tsp (15 mL) salt
2 eggs
1 tbsp plus 1 tsp (20 mL) sour cream
⅔ cup (185 mL) water
sour cream, for serving
sliced spring onions, for garnish (optional)

Caramelized Onions

8 cups (2 L) sliced onions
1 tbsp (15 mL) olive oil
3 tbsp (45 mL) butter
¼ tsp (1 mL) salt
¼ tsp (1 mL) pepper

For the perogy filling:

Preheat barbecue on high. Season bison hump with salt and pepper and sear on all sides until meat is nicely charred. Place in a roasting pan with enough room to submerge with the wine and bison (or beef) stock.

Add onion, celery, carrot, garlic, vinegar, bay leaf, peppercorns, juniper berries and herbs. Bring to a gentle simmer on the stove. Cover the pan and place in a preheated 330°F (165°C) oven. Cook for about 3 hours, or until meat is fork-tender. Carefully remove bison from stock and allow to cool, wrapped tightly in plastic (braised meats dry out very easily so refrain from leaving it uncovered).

Strain braising stock and begin to reduce it, occasionally skimming to remove any fat. Reduced sauce should be dark and rich, about 1 cup (250 mL) in volume. Add Saskatoon berries to liquid along with half the caramelized onions. Bring just to a simmer and set aside.

Shred cooked bison meat and add it to reduced stock. Heat through and season if needed, then cool completely so that it sets up quite solid. The filling needs to be easy to roll into balls when refrigerated. This will make forming the perogies easier.

For the dough:

Mix dry ingredients in one bowl. Mix wet ingredients in a second bowl. Add wet to dry and combine until a moist dough forms. Dump onto a floured work surface and knead until dough is smooth. Rest for several hours or overnight if possible before rolling.

Roll out dough and cut into 3-in (7.5-cm) circles. Place a spoonful of bison mixture on each round and fold in half, sealing the edge by pinching the sides together. Drop perogies into salted boiling water a few at a time and cook until they float, then another minute. Remove from water and drain well.

Quickly fry perogies with a little more caramelized onion and serve with sour cream and a garnish of sliced spring onions.

Yields about 50 perogies

For the caramelized onions:

Place all ingredients in a heavy-bottomed pan. Cover and place over medium-low heat. Cook until onions are very tender, stirring occasionally. When onions are tender, about 20 minutes, remove the cover and continue to cook until golden brown.

Yields about 1 to 1 ½ cups (250 to 375 mL)

Fish &
Shellfish

When we think of Canadian seafood we tend to think of British Columbia and the Atlantic provinces. Certainly the bounty of Canada's Atlantic and Pacific fishing grounds is amazing, but the Great Lakes and the waters of Canada's north have provided chefs with fish varieties like lake trout, pike, pickerel, bass and Arctic char, to name but a few. The world of aquaculture has reduced our reliance on seasonal fisheries by providing many species year round. And sustainable seafood practices are becoming more and more common as consumers become aware of the impacts of irresponsible harvesting within our waters.

Fish has been consumed more than any other source of protein in human history. There is a feeling of satisfaction that comes from eating something that is good for us, and in sharing the experience with those around us. No matter what culture we belong to we can identify with seafood in our diets. We are also more flexible about our seafood, allowing new ethnic recipes onto our menus and into our own culture. Certainly in Canada, a true melting pot, we expect to see foreign influences in our food. Imagine Vancouver or Halifax without Japanese sushi, or cured Solomon Gundy and salmon inspired by Norwegian immigrants, or fish 'n' chips, a distinctly British invention.

But in the traditional bistros of Southern France, as in our own bistros in Canada, the menu is most influenced by what has been caught that very day, together with what is on hand and what can be paired with it. Fish must be properly cooked — just cooked in most cases — and seasoned in a way that allows the subtle flavours of the ocean to come through. Cooking fish and seafood demands a great deal of respect and technique from the cook, and in this chapter you will see how the chefs showcase some of Canada's greatest and most historically important ingredients.

Rhubarb Glazed Scallops

Paul McInnis, Rhubarb Grill and Café, Indian Harbour, Nova Scotia

Located along one of the most beautiful stretches of road in Canada, Rhubarb Grill is an elegant oasis serving fresh, local ingredients on a small but sophisticated bistro-style menu. As you would expect, chef and owner Paul McInnis has a lot of fun with rhubarb. The nature of cooked rhubarb is its tanginess and pleasing acidity. When balanced with some form of sugar and complementary spices, rhubarb's unique flavour actually becomes more pronounced. This is Paul's signature scallop dish. It uses a unique glaze and can be served as an appetizer or as a main course with a little extra glaze, a sauté of julienned vegetables and some simple steamed rice. Paul also recommends the glaze as a dipping sauce for spring rolls, as a substitute for barbecue sauce or even over vanilla ice cream.

Rhubarb Glaze
8 oz (225g) fresh rhubarb, chopped
8 oz (225g) tamarind paste (break into small chunks if necessary)
2 cups (500 mL) mirin (seasoned rice wine)
2 cups (500 mL) brown sugar
3 kaffir lime leaves, roughly chopped or crushed
3 stalks fresh lemon grass, roughly chopped

Scallops
12 large sea scallops (under 10 per pound count)
2 tbsp (30 mL) organic canola oil
¼ cup (60 mL) Rhubarb Glaze

For the glaze:
Combine all ingredients in a saucepan and simmer slowly over medium-low heat, stirring often, until it forms a thick syrupy texture (approximately 30 minutes). Press through a sieve to remove pulp and pit, using a rubber spatula. Store in a sealed Mason jar, refrigerated, for up to 1 month, or sterilize using a standard bottling procedure.

Yields 2 cups (500 mL)

For the scallops:
Preheat oven to 400°F (200°C). Pat sea scallops dry with a clean towel. Preheat a cast iron skillet (or stainless steel frying pan) until it begins to smoke. Add oil and place each scallop in the pan with the flat side down. Cook scallops on one side without disturbing them for 90 seconds, or until they show a little bit of caramel-coloured golden brown on the sides. Flip scallops in pan, drizzle with Rhubarb Glaze, and place in oven for 2 minutes, or until desired doneness is achieved.

Serves 4 as an appetizer, 2 as a main course

Pan-roasted Atlantic Cod with Jerusalem Artichoke Mash, Spinach and Green Onion Oil

Dennis Johnston, Fid, Halifax, Nova Scotia

Dennis Johnston is one of the very first chefs in Nova Scotia to vigorously promote locally sourced and grown ingredients. His menus proudly feature the names of the farms that produce his unique dishes. In this dish, simple Grand Manan cod fillets are cooked in his signature French style, *à l'unilateral*, a term for cooking proteins, particularly fish, on one side in a pan. This creates three contrasting textures in the fish: a superb crust on the seared side, a gently cooked interior and a barely cooked or "cool" bottom. Dennis's dish is the essence of simple bistro cooking, using the freshest possible ingredients and cooking them well. The East Coast inspiration to this dish, one of fried fish, potato mash and wilted greens makes it one of my favourites.

Jerusalem Artichoke Mash
1 lb (450 g) Jerusalem artichokes
1 tbsp (15 mL) sea salt
2 tbsp (30 mL) butter
a few grindings of fresh black pepper

Green Onion Oil
4 green onion tops, coarsely chopped
½ cup (125 mL) canola oil
pinch of salt

Pan-roasted Cod
4 x 6-oz (170-g) Atlantic cod fillets
sea salt and pepper, to taste
olive oil to cover bottom of a frying pan

Spinach
6 cups (4 large handfuls) organic spinach
sea salt and pepper to taste
¼ cup (60 mL) pomegranate seeds (for garnish)

For the mash:
Peel Jerusalem artichokes, place them in a small pot with three large pinches of salt and cover with cold water. Bring to a simmer and cook until fork tender.

Strain and mash with a potato masher. Add butter and season with black pepper. The mash can be prepared ahead of time and reheated before serving.

For the green onion oil:
Simply purée onion tops in oil until smooth, and season with a little salt. Pour into a small bowl and reserve.

For the cod:
Preheat a frying pan until hot and pat fish dry with a paper towel. Season each side with a little salt and pepper. Add oil to the pan and when a small amount of smoke begins to curl upwards, place fish carefully in the pan. Reduce the heat to medium and cook fish entirely on one side. Do not flip it at any point. The fillet will slowly cook through in about 6 to 7 minutes.

For the spinach:
Pick off any larger, woody stems from spinach leaves. Wash thoroughly (organic spinach is often sandy) and spin in a lettuce spinner to dry. Steam spinach over a double boiler until wilted and tender, then season with salt and pepper.

Presentation:
Place a small pile of warm Jerusalem artichoke mash in the centre of a white dinner plate. Place a pile of spinach on top of mash and then carefully place cod, seared side up, on spinach. Using a teaspoon, drizzle a circle of green onion oil around the dish and sprinkle with a few pomegranate seeds.

Serves 4

Shellfish and Summer Vegetable "Hodge Podge"

Hodge podge is a classic Maritime dish that uses the very first garden vegetables of the year. On its own it's a treat every year. The addition of the very best shellfish makes it unique and sophisticated, yet still bistro in essence. It can be served alone as an appetizer or as an accompaniment to a fillet of roasted halibut, trout or salmon. I like to fry small golden and red beets, making little coins of crisp and colourful confetti for garnish, so that I can include beets in the dish without the creamy white sauce turning colour.

1 lb (450 g) baby new potatoes (cleaned but unpeeled)
8 oz (225 g) baby carrots
1 cup (250 mL) shelled fresh peas
4 tbsp (60 mL) salted butter
1 clove garlic, minced
1 shallot, minced
½ tsp (3 mL) sea salt
1/2 tsp (3 mL) freshly ground black pepper
2 tbsp (30 mL) vermouth or white wine
½ cup (125 mL) chicken broth
1 cup (250 mL) 35% cream
¼ cup (60 mL) creamy fresh goat's cheese
½ cup (125 mL) chunked fresh-cooked snow crab meat
½ cup (125 mL) chunked fresh-cooked lobster meat
½ cup (125 mL) steamed and shucked fresh mussels
12 oysters, freshly shucked with liquor reserved
¼ cup (60 mL) freshly chopped chives
3 tbsp (45 mL) extra-virgin olive oil
12 large sea scallops
1 cup (250 mL) small arugula leaves
6 ripe cherry tomatoes

In a pot of salted water, cook baby new potatoes until soft. Cut potatoes in half. Blanch whole carrots in the same water and set aside. Blanch peas in the water as well, and shock in iced water to prevent them from continuing to cook.

In a large saucepan, heat butter and sauté garlic and shallot for 1 minute until shallot is translucent. Return potatoes, carrots and peas to the saucepan and season with salt and pepper. Deglaze pan with vermouth (or white wine) and add chicken broth and cream. Bring to a boil and add goat's cheese, stirring well to make sauce smooth. Reduce sauce by one-third. Add crab, lobster, mussels, oysters, oyster liquor and chopped chives.

In a separate sauté pan, heat olive oil and sear scallops on flat side. Do not move scallops for at least 90 seconds, allowing them to caramelize well. When golden brown, flip them and cook for 90 seconds on second side.

To plate the dish, warm 6 plates in the oven. Spoon hodge podge onto the plate, allowing it to spread out and show off all the vegetables and seafood in the sauce. Place two sea scallops on top of each portion and garnish with several small arugula leaves and a few slices of cherry tomatoes.

Serves 6, as a main course

Butter-roasted Halibut with Asparagus "Noodles" and Beurre Blanc

In great bistros, fish dishes usually take a just-caught piece of seafood, cook it at the very last minute and accompany it with something fresh and light, often a vegetable. The beauty of this recipe is that it follows this path by taking a few simple ingredients, at the peak of freshness, and elevating them into an elegant dish. The key here is to find the right cut of halibut and to follow the method of butter-basting it in the pan. Ask your fishmonger for a thick-cut, boneless halibut loin from the centre of the fish, away from the tail. This makes the fish a bit sturdier in the pan and prevents it from overcooking and crumbling. The beurre blanc can be made just before you start the fish and held warm until you are ready to serve.

Asparagus "Noodles"

2 lb (1 kg) fresh asparagus
1 tbsp (15 mL) chopped flatleaf parsley
1 tsp (5 mL) chopped fresh tarragon
1 tsp (5 mL) chopped thyme leaves
salt and pepper

Butter-roasted Halibut

3 lb (1.5 kg) boneless halibut loin (cut into 6 x 8-oz/250-g portions)
3 tbsp (45 mL) olive or vegetable oil
1 cup (250 mL) melted butter
zest of ½ lemon
coarse sea salt
freshly ground black pepper

Beurre Blanc

1 shallot, minced
1 bay leaf
1 sprig thyme
6 black peppercorns (optional)
juice of ½ lemon
½ cup (125 mL) dry vermouth
¼ cup (60 mL) white wine vinegar
2 tbsp (30 mL) 35% cream
1 cup (250 mL) cold salted butter (cut into tablespoon-sized cubes)
sliced chives for garnish

For the "noodles":

Prepare asparagus by removing bottom 2 in (5 cm) of stalk. Using a vegetable peeler or mandolin slicer, cut each asparagus stalk lengthwise into ribbons. Each ribbon will be approximately 5 or 6 in (13 or 15 cm) in length. Bring a large pot of salted water to the boil and set asparagus aside until fish and beurre blanc recipes are ready.

Drop asparagus ribbons into boiling water and cook for 2 minutes until just soft. Remove from water using a spider or pair of tongs, place in a bowl and toss with parsley, tarragon, thyme leaves and about 2 tablespoons of butter from the halibut pan. Season with a little salt and pepper if desired.

For the halibut:

Preheat a skillet over medium-high heat. Add oil and sear presentation side (usually the side of the fillet opposite the skin side) of halibut for 2 minutes, until slightly browned. Reduce the heat to low and add butter and lemon zest. Using a serving spoon, baste halibut fillets with butter. Continue doing this for about 8 minutes, flipping fish once or twice in the pan along the way. When fish is firm to the touch, remove from the heat and let stand for 3 minutes, presentation side up. Sprinkle with sea salt and freshly ground black pepper.

For the beurre blanc:

In a saucepan, combine shallot, bay leaf, thyme, peppercorns, lemon juice, vermouth and vinegar and bring to a boil. Reduce liquid until only ¼ cup (60 mL) remains. Strain reduction into a clean saucepan and discard shallots and herbs. Add cream and just bring back to a simmer. Begin whisking in cold butter while reduction is over very low heat, a cube or two at a time, until sauce begins to thicken. When only one cube of butter remains, remove sauce from the heat and whisk the last one in to the side of the stove. If you are using unsalted butter you may need to adjust seasoning at this stage. Do not boil the beurre blanc after the emulsion has formed or the sauce will break.

Presentation:

Make a mound of asparagus in the centre of a pasta bowl, as you would with linguini or spaghetti noodles. Place a piece of fish on top and then pour a couple of spoonfuls of beurre blanc over the top. Garnish with sliced chives.

Serves 6

Crispy B.C. Sardines with New Potatoes, Green Beans and Maple Mustard Vinaigrette

Robert Clark, Raincity Grill, Vancouver, British Columbia

Chef Clark has always endorsed sustainable fisheries and the B.C. sardine industry is well on its way to once again becoming the thriving success it once was. Fresh sardines are much larger than you might think, and this recipe is not referring to the canned variety. The fillets can be 6 to 9 inches (15 to 23 cm) in length or even larger. Robert presents this as a great summer hot dish, but says the fish can also be made in advance, put in a shallow dish or casserole and served with the dressing cold over the top. It makes a wonderful summer *antipasti* on the deck and réminds me of dining *alfresco* on a bistro patio in southern France.

Sardines

6 whole, fresh B.C. sardines
1 tbsp (15 mL) maple syrup
1 tbsp (15 mL) kosher salt
freshly ground pepper
1 cup (250 mL) panko breadcrumbs
3 tbsp (45 mL) good olive oil

Potato and Bean Salad

1 lb (450 g) little new potatoes
¼ tsp (1 mL) salt
8 oz (225 g) French "filet" beans (green beans)
3 tbsp (45 mL) butter, melted
2 tbsp (30 mL) tarragon vinegar
1 tbsp (15 mL) chopped parsley
1 tsp (5 mL) salt
½ tsp (3 mL) pepper

Maple Mustard Vinaigrette

¼ cup (60 mL) sliced shallots
1 garlic clove, sliced
1 tbsp (15 mL) good olive oil
¼ cup (60 mL) finely diced red bell pepper
½ cup (125 mL) dry white wine
2 tbsp (30 mL) maple syrup
3 tbsp (45 mL) seasoned rice wine vinegar
2 tsp (10 mL) Dijon mustard
4 tbsp (60 mL) good olive oil (second amount)

For the fish:

Fillet sardines, rinse in cold water and pat dry. Lay fillets side by side on a tray with exposed flesh facing up. Brush sardines with maple syrup and season with salt and pepper. Allow fish to sit for 1 hour. Coat fillets in breadcrumbs and fry in olive oil over medium heat until golden brown, about 2 minutes on each side. Remove from the pan and reserve.

For the salad:

Wash, but do not peel, new potatoes. Boil in salted water until fork-tender. In a separate pot or steamer, blanch filet beans until they are just crisp and vibrant green, about 2 minutes. To serve this simple salad warm, toss potatoes and beans in melted butter, vinegar, parsley and seasonings. Serve immediately.

For the vinaigrette:

Sauté shallots and garlic in olive oil for 3 minutes. Add peppers, white wine, maple syrup and vinegar and reduce mixture by half on high heat. Finish sauce by whisking in mustard and olive oil. Adjust seasoning with a little salt and pepper if needed.

Presentation:

Make a pile of bean and potato salad in the centre of a plate or bowl. Place crispy fish on salad and pour the warm sauce over top.

Serves 6

Penne with Smoked Salmon and Cream Cheese Sauce

Michael Smith, Food Network Canada, Fortune, Prince Edward Island

Michael loves cooking for his family and has found numerous ways to speed up the process of making dishes from scratch. "This is my family's all-time favourite dinner party pasta dish," he notes. "Our friends request it all the time. It's easy to make too, because it makes its own sauce! You can toss steaming wet, just-cooked pasta with melting cream cheese to form an incredibly smooth luxurious sauce. The smoked salmon adds extravagance balanced by other familiar flavours: dill, lemon, onion, mustard and capers." If you have the time, smoking your own salmon on the barbecue is fun and makes this dish extra special, but with so many great Canadian smokehouses, high quality smoked fish is available almost everywhere.

1 lb (450 g) dry penne pasta

2 cups (500 mL) cream cheese at room temperature

¼ cup (60 mL) chopped fresh dill

4 green onions, thinly sliced

juice and zest of 1 lemon

1 tbsp plus 1 tsp (20 mL) Dijon mustard

¼ cup (60 mL) capers

1 lb (450 g) hot-smoked salmon, flaked (or cold-smoked salmon cut into ribbons)

½ tsp (3 mL) salt

½ tsp (3 mL) freshly ground black pepper

Bring a large pot of water to the boil. Season it liberally with salt until it tastes like seawater. When it is boiling furiously, add the pasta. Cook to al dente, until the pasta is cooked through but still pleasantly chewy (approximately 7 minutes).

Scoop out some of the starchy cooking water and reserve. Drain pasta but not quite all the way — leave it a bit wet. Return pasta to the pot, along with a splash or two of the reserved water, perhaps ¾ of a cup (185 mL) or so in total.

While pasta is still steaming hot immediately add all remaining ingredients except salmon and seasonings. Stir with a wooden spoon as cheese melts and forms a creamy sauce. At the last second, briefly fold in smoked salmon so it won't break up too much. Season with salt and pepper and serve immediately.

Serves 4

Smoked Wild Arctic Char, Crab and Asparagus Wraps

Ray Lovell, Golden Palate, Jasper, Alberta

Ray's "wrap" is an extremely versatile dish, especially when entertaining. These little wraps, as the chef suggests, can be served chilled as an appetizer, quickly grilled over a barbecue, or steamed just before serving. Arctic char is a wonderful fish with plenty of flavour and a vibrant colour, and it is often farmed sustainably. Smoked Arctic char is becoming easier to find in local smokehouses across the country, but if you cannot find any you can certainly substitute smoked salmon or even halibut. For me this a wonderful bistro starter. It is not too filling and wakens the palate for the main course to come.

1 cup (250 mL) cooked snow crab meat

zest and juice of ½ lemon

zest and juice of ½ lime

1 tbsp (15 mL) freshly snipped chives

1 tsp (5 mL) fresh dill

1 x 10-oz (300-g) package softened cream cheese

½ cup (125 mL) 35% cream

salt and pepper to taste

6 slices (6-in / 15-cm) double-smoked wild arctic char
   (cold-smoked)

18 pieces (approximately 1 lb / 450 g) fresh pencil
   asparagus, blanched and cooled

Combine crab meat, lemon and lime juice, chives, dill and ½ of the grated zest and mix well. In a stand mixer whip cream cheese and cream together, until smooth and slightly fluffy. Fold marinated crabmeat into cheese and season with a little salt and freshly ground black pepper. Refrigerate until ready to assemble wraps.

Lay a slice of char on a flat surface and spread with an even layer (about ¼-in/5-mm thick) of crabmeat mix. Place 3 spears of asparagus onto crabmeat and roll. Depending on the size of the fish slices, it may be necessary to use 2 slices to complete a full roll.

Serves 6

Warm Lake Erie Yellow Perch with Cauliflower Velouté and Rainbow Chard

Anthony Walsh, Canoe, Toronto, Ontario

Anthony Walsh could be the busiest chef in Canada, running about a half a dozen of the best restaurants in Toronto. It is at Canoe where Anthony's Canadian cuisine is most prominently showcased. Having worked in the Canoe kitchen and eaten dozens of his dishes, what always struck me was how "bistro" Anthony's food truly was. Every day he cooks food that is rooted in history, home cooking and simple freshness. Behind each taste experience in that restaurant is Anthony's dedication to the pursuit of a perfect piece of gnocchi, a tender piece of braised pork belly, or an examination of all things *mushroom*. This dish shows how elegant, stunning or "flashy" food can be made with some great fresh fish, wilted greens and a new way of cooking cauliflower. It is food we have all eaten, flavours we identify with and find altogether comforting. It is what "bistro" means.

Fish

8 x 2-oz (60-g) skinless, boneless fillets of yellow perch
5 tbsp (75 mL) extra-virgin olive oil
zest of 1/2 lemon
1 tsp (5 mL) freshly picked thyme leaves
½ tsp (3 mL) Maldon sea salt
1 cup (250 mL) minced raw cauliflower
1 cup (250 mL) 35% cream
¼ cup (60 mL) minced shallot
½ tsp (3 mL) ground nutmeg
1 fresh bay leaf
½ bunch rainbow chard (about 1 lb)
1 tbsp (15 mL) Chardonnay
1 tbsp (15 mL) crème fraîche
¼ cup (60 mL) olive oil

Sauce

2 tbsp (30 mL) minced shallot
⅓ cup (85 mL) minced white of leek
1 tbsp (15 mL) butter
1 cup (250 mL) Chardonnay (approximately)
1 fresh bay leaf
⅓ cup (85 mL) crème fraîche
2 tbsp (30 mL) Pelee Island whitefish caviar

For the fish:

Dress fish with olive oil, lemon zest, thyme leaves and a pinch of Maldon salt. Place seasoned fish in a very low oven, at 175°F (80°C), for 12 to 15 minutes.

In a saucepan, place cauliflower in cream with shallot, nutmeg, bay leaf and a pinch of salt. Cover and simmer over medium heat until cauliflower is tender. Process cauliflower in a blender until silky smooth. Keep warm.

Clean and remove stems from chard leaves and cut into 3-in (7.5-cm) batons. Cut larger pieces lengthwise if needed. In boiling salted water, blanch stem batons for 1 minute and refresh in iced water. Remove from iced water and dress lightly with a tablespoon of wine, a pinch of salt and olive oil.

In the same boiling water, blanch chard leaves for 2 minutes then shock in iced water. Place leaves in a blender along with first amount of crème fraîche and process briefly until coarsely puréed. Adjust seasonings with a little salt and pepper.

Warm chard batons and purée.

For the sauce:

In a small pot, sweat second amount of shallots and leeks with butter until soft, with no colour. Add bay leaf and deglaze mixture with approximately 1 cup wine. Reduce by two-thirds, add crème fraîche and process until smooth, adjusting seasonings to your personal taste.

Presentation:

Place a heaping spoonful of the cauliflower purée in the centre of a warm plate or pasta bowl. Using the back of the spoon, make a "well" in the centre. Place a mound of chard leaves in well. Gently place warm perch fillets atop purées and add seasoned chard stems on top and around perch. Finally, drizzle warm sauce around perch and place a healthy mound of caviar in and around sauce.

Serves 8

Pan-roasted Trout with Vegetable Bubbles

Paul Rogalski, Rouge, Calgary, Alberta

Paul pushes the norms of Canadian cuisine. He is a chef who moves within a world of local and seasonal producers but uses both traditional and modern cooking techniques in his dishes. The recipe below may be your first foray into the world we chefs call "molecular gastronomy," but I challenge you to give it a try. I believe you will discover that it is a way of cooking that endeavours to bring new textures and ideas to food, but treats the ingredients with absolute respect. Isolating and enhancing the flavour profile of an ingredient can only be successful when the ingredient is at its very best. "Feel free to change the vegetable juice for making the bubbles," notes Paul. "You can always add some chopped herbs from your garden too."

Vegetable Bubbles

2 tbsp (30 mL) agar powder

½ cup (125 mL) red bell pepper juice (seasoned to taste)

6 cups (1.5 L) canola oil (chilled in a deep freeze to -15°F/ -25°C)

½ cup (125 mL) cucumber juice (seasoned to taste)

¼ cup (60 mL) freshly shelled pea pearls

Trout

3 whole trout, filleted (about 1 ½ lb/675 g each)

2 tbsp (30 mL) unsalted butter

2 medium onions, diced small

4 celery stalks, diced small

1 bulb anise, diced medium

1 white of leek (cut lengthwise, washed then diced medium)

2 tbsp (30 mL) finely chopped ginger

1 stalk lemongrass, cleaned and thinly sliced

¼ cup (60 mL) roughly chopped fresh flatleaf parsley (leaves and stems)

6 sprigs fresh thyme

2 tbsp (30 mL) whole black peppercorns

1 tsp (5 mL) sea salt

½ cup (125 mL) white wine (Gewürztraminer or Riesling)

8 cups (2 L) very cold water

2 tbsp (30 mL) olive oil

2 tbsp (30 mL) butter (second amount)

For the bubbles:

Soften 1 tbsp (15 mL) of agar in 3 tbsp (45 mL) of red bell pepper juice at room temperature. Meanwhile, heat remaining bell pepper juice to a simmer. Pour agar/juice mix into simmering juice, dissolve completely, return to a simmer and immediately remove from the heat. Using a large syringe, gather mixture and slowly drip into frozen canola oil, allowing pearls to form. Continue until mixture is finished. Harvest pearls with a wire mesh scoop and rinse with cold water. Refrigerate for future use.

Refreeze canola oil and repeat method with cucumber juice.

For the trout:

To fillet, run a knife under the gill and along the backbone, removing the fillet in one long swipe of the knife. If you aren't feeling adventurous, ask your fishmonger to do it for you, saving the bones and fillets separately. Portion trout fillets into 6-oz (180-g) pieces, or about half a fillet per person. Remove pin bones with a small pair of pliers if desired, but it is not necessary: just be careful when eating the fish if you do not take them out. Refrigerate fillets until ready to cook. Wash fish bones and heads under cold water before continuing with the stock.

Melt butter in a heavy 7- to 8-quart (7- to 8-L) stockpot, over medium heat. Add all vegetables, ginger, lemongrass, parsley, thyme and peppercorns. Cook until vegetables become transparent. Stir frequently to avoid browning.

Place trout bones evenly on top of vegetables. Add salt, wine and enough water to just cover bones. Bring stock to a simmer over high heat. Reduce heat to low as soon as a soft simmer has been achieved. Carefully remove foam or scum from top of stock as it simmers, and continue cooking for 30 minutes. Do not disturb stock by stirring or shaking or it may become cloudy.

Carefully siphon or strain stock through a very fine mesh strainer or cheesecloth into another stockpot or heatproof container. Agitate bones as little as possible. Season to taste. Use immediately for best aromatics.

Heat a nonstick pan over medium-high heat. Using a sharp knife, cut 3 slits in skin of trout, about ¼ in (5 smm) deep. Sear fish in a small quantity of olive oil for 3 minutes on the skin side or until it is crispy. Flip fish onto the other side, remove from the heat, and add butter. Allow fish to complete its cooking using only the residual heat from the pan. Rest for 4 minutes until ready to serve.

To serve, distribute vegetable bubbles in white soup plates or pasta bowls. Simmer trout broth, add shelled peas and cook for 1 minute. Remove peas and divide into serving bowls. Ladle more hot broth into each bowl and place trout fillet, crispy skin side up, in the bowl. Garnish with some fresh herbs and a little sea salt on the fish skin.

Serves 8 to 10

Seafood Risotto

Fresh Canadian seafood is a passion of mine, as is risotto-making. When I make this dish I follow the criteria for a French *bouillabaisse* or any quality seafood stew: worry less about the fish or shellfish you see in the recipe and more about what you can get absolutely fresh. So, take this recipe as a guide. If you happen across incredible sea scallops and beautiful white cod, use them. Or maybe you have a friend who knows a lobster fisherman. There is one exception: I do like to use canned baby clams as I find them great in the broth itself. I also simmer the broth first with dulse from New Brunswick as it has the taste of *umami*, which boosts the subtle oceanic flavour in the risotto. Raw lobster meat is available in good fish shops in small, vacuum-packed bags, but using cooked tails is acceptable in a pinch.

3 cups (750 mL) low-sodium chicken broth
1 cup (250 mL) clam juice
liquid reserved from drained clams (see below)
3 or 4 pieces dulse
2 shallots, minced
1 clove garlic, minced
¼ bulb fennel, minced
½ tsp (3 mL) freshly ground black pepper
¼ cup (60 mL) extra-virgin olive oil
1 cup (250 mL) Italian Arborio or Caranoli rice
½ cup (125 mL) dry vermouth
1 x 8-oz (225-g) haddock, cod or hake fillet
1 cup (250 mL) cooked and chunked king or snow crab meat
1 cup (250 mL) steamed and shucked mussels
½ cup (125 mL) coldwater shrimp
2 small cans (10 oz total) baby clams, drained (liquid reserved)
16 in-shell live scallops (or 16 large sea scallops out of the shell)
4 raw lobster tails, sliced lengthwise (8 pieces total)
½ cup (125 mL) cream cheese
¼ cup (60 mL) chopped Italian parsley
¼ cup (60 mL) cubed butter

In a stockpot, simmer chicken broth, clam juice, liquid from drained baby clams and dulse for at least 30 minutes before making the risotto. Remove dulse and discard.

In a separate heavy-bottomed stockpot, sauté shallots, garlic, fennel and pepper in olive oil over medium heat for 5 minutes, until soft and translucent. Add rice and stir well to coat in the oil. Cook for 2 minutes until rice looks translucent. Add vermouth and cook out liquid completely. Add one ladle of broth to the rice and stir gently, cooking until liquid is gone and the rice looks dry. Add a second ladle and do this again. Repeat this process, all the while stirring the rice gently. After 10 minutes of adding broth, add haddock (or white-fleshed fish of choice), resting it on top of rice. Reduce the heat to low and cover the pot. Steam for 3 minutes or so, remove the lid and add another ladle of hot broth. Stir rice again and gently break up the fish as you do so, distributing small flakes of fish throughout the rice. Add crab, mussels, shrimp and clams, along with remaining broth. Stir through the rice and then place in-shell scallops and lobster tails on top of rice. Do not stir them through but cover the pot again. Steam for 5 minutes over low heat. When scallops open, remove them from the pan, along with lobster tails. Set aside to garnish each portion of risotto.

Add cream cheese, parsley and butter and stir into rice. The rice will be cooked in about 18 minutes from the time you added the first liquid. For a soupier risotto it may be necessary to add another ½ cup (125 mL) of chicken stock at the end. Adjust the salt to taste as many stocks and clam juice products available at the market have a high sodium content.

Presentation:
Spoon risotto into pasta bowls and garnish each portion with 2 scallops and a lobster tail. Drizzle with a small amount of extra-virgin olive oil and some chopped parsley or chives if desired. Risotto does not keep well, so serve immediately.

Serves 8

Barbecued Stuffed Trout with Smoked Potato Salad

Whole trout can be stuffed with anything you like, but here I am using classic seafood pairings like fennel and lemon. Many whole-fish recipes call for wrapping the fish in parchment or foil to keep in the moisture. I prefer to treat this dish as if I were camping in the woods: rustic and slightly charred so it réminds me of summer even when the snow is flying. The smoked potato salad is a new and interesting twist on a picnic staple. It goes well with just about anything from the barbecue, and potatoes are available all year long.

Trout

1 x 2-to-3-lb (900- to 1350-g) whole trout, head on and
    entrails removed
salt and pepper
1 lemon, sliced into ¼-in (5-mm) rounds
¼ bulb fennel with green tops, sliced
6 sprigs fresh thyme
2 cloves garlic

Smoked Potato Salad

2 lb (900 g) baby red or white new potatoes
1 small red onion, minced
½ cup (125 mL) bread and butter pickles
3 tbsp (45 mL) bread and butter pickle juice
1 cup (250 mL) real mayonnaise
1 tbsp (15 mL) Dijon mustard
2 hardboiled eggs, chopped
1 tbsp (15 mL) fresh tarragon, chopped
2 tbsp (30 mL) fresh Italian parsley, chopped
½ tsp (3 mL) sea salt
juice and zest of ½ lemon
½ tsp (3 mL) freshly ground black pepper
a dash of hot sauce such as Tabasco

For the trout:

Wash body cavity of trout thoroughly under running water, and pat dry with paper towels. Season cavity with salt and pepper and stuff with remaining ingredients, without too much fussing. Tie a couple of loops of butcher's twine around fish to keep the stuffing inside during grilling.

If using charcoal, wait until the flame has subsided completely and the coals are red embers. Rub fish with a tiny bit of oil and grill for about 7 minutes on each side (depending on the intensity of the heat — some cook's discretion is needed here). When just cooked through, remove string, peel back skin, and use a spoon to scoop the moist meat from the bony carcass.

Season with a little salt and pepper before serving.

For the potato salad:

Cook potatoes completely in salted water until tender. Before smoking, cool and slice each potato in half, exposing the flesh inside. Using a stovetop smoker or barbecue, place ½ cup (125 mL) of cooking grade woodchips in a smoking pouch and set them on the burner. (The barbecue section of your local hardware store will have all the woodchips, foil pouches and instructions you need.) When potatoes have smoked for at least 10 minutes in direct smoke, remove and rest them for 24 hours.

The next day, mix potatoes together with all remaining ingredients.

Note: If making this salad all in one day, smoke potatoes for half the time. Resting smoked foods overnight allows the harshness to subside and prevents a bitter flavour from coming through. Very lightly smoked foods do not need the same amount of rest.

Serves 6, with leftovers

Meat, Poultry & Game

Enter a stuffy and pretentious fine-dining restaurant 30 years ago and you would likely find a menu offering a neat and tidy rack of lamb, filet mignon or supreme of chicken breast stuffed with crab. But travel onto the side streets of a European city or drive into a small village and you would find a different sort of offering in bistros, quaint little restaurants and pubs. In these establishments the cooking heritage of the region was displayed in its peasant dishes, the foods the common person ate. Money was tight and meat was a real treat. On the farm, animals were raised for a purpose and nothing was wasted. Lesser cuts were used as they cost less, resulting in a rich and delicious variety of braised dishes. Offal meats were transformed into supper and served with homemade wine. Eventually these simple peasant recipes became tradition; they were jotted down on recipe cards and taught to the next generation. Some even made their way into the curriculum of culinary schools.

Enter some of those very same restaurants today, especially in this country, and you will see that the simplest meat preparations are back in fashion. The most brilliant chefs around the world have come to realize that there is true beauty and sophistication in a succulent piece of braised lamb, and that serving secondary cuts is cost-effective and responsible. If we as a culture consumed only the "pretty" cuts like tenderloin, New York strips and boneless chicken breasts, imagine how much would be wasted.

This chapter will introduce you to a wide range of meat, poultry and game dishes that use cuts of meat both common and seldom used. However, almost all are attainable by speaking to your local butcher in advance. Give them a try and experience true Canadian bistro cooking at its best.

Glazed Lamb Shanks with Simply Perfect Risotto

This is my favourite "bistro" dish. It is unbelievably flavourful, rich and rooted in culinary history. I have always been a passionate student of risotto-making and I think this one rivals any I have ever made. Nova Scotia lamb is among the best in the world, but as long as you choose locally raised, grass-fed lamb, your end result will be every bit as good. Making a simple lamb broth with a pound of bones from your butcher is well worth the effort for this recipe, but beef broth is a good substitute.

Lamb

2 heads garlic
6 lamb shanks (about 12 oz/340 g each)
½ cup (125 mL) bacon or duck fat (vegetable oil is fine)
2 onions, coarsely chopped
2 stalks celery, coarsely chopped
2 medium-sized carrots, coarsely chopped
2 cups (500 mL) dry sherry
2 cups (500 mL) medium-bodied red wine (Merlot or Shiraz)
2 cups (500 mL) lamb broth
6 sprigs fresh thyme
4 sprigs fresh mint
4 bay leaves
salt and pepper, to season

Risotto

1 medium onion, minced
1 clove garlic, minced
½ tsp (3 mL) salt
½ tsp (3 mL) freshly ground black pepper
2 tbsp (30 mL) extra-virgin olive oil
1 cup (250 mL) Caranoli rice
½ cup (125 mL) dry vermouth
3 ½ cups (875 mL) hot chicken broth
½ cup (125 mL) grated Parmigiano-Reggiano cheese
2 tbsp (30 mL) butter

For the lamb:

In an oven preheated to 350°F (180°C), roast garlic heads in aluminum foil for 30 to 40 minutes. Allow to cool and squeeze soft cloves out of the papery skins. Smash roughly with a fork and set aside.

Pan-roast lamb shanks in bacon or duck fat until golden brown on all sides. Remove from the pan and place in a braising dish or steep-sided roasting pan. Remove excess fat from pan, then sauté onions, celery and carrots for 10 minutes, until slightly caramelized. Deglaze the pan with sherry. Add all vegetables, wine, broth, herbs and roasted garlic to the braising dish. There should be enough liquid to completely cover the shanks.

Bring to the boil and transfer to a 300°F (150°C) oven and braise, covered, for 2 ½ to 3 hours. Remove from oven and let shanks set in braising liquor for 1 hour. Remove shanks to a second ovenproof pan, cover with plastic wrap and set in a warm place. Strain braising liquor into a sauce pan and reduce over medium heat by two-thirds, until sauce will coat the back of a wooden spoon. Season sauce with a little salt and pepper *after* the reduction is complete to ensure that it is not too salty.

Ladle some sauce over shanks and place in a 350°F (180°C) oven for 5 to 7 minutes to reheat before serving. The sauce will glaze the shanks as they reheat. Carefully remove from the pan with a slotted spoon.

For the risotto:

In a heavy-bottomed sauté pan, sauté onion, garlic, salt and pepper over medium heat in olive oil for 5 minutes or until soft. Add rice and cook for 3 minutes on medium heat until grains look translucent. Deglaze pan with vermouth and cook until the bottom of the pan is dry or *au sec*. Begin adding hot broth one 8-oz (225-mL) ladle at a time, stirring constantly. The risotto will take about 15 to 18 minutes to cook depending on the variety of rice. When risotto is fully cooked but still *al dente* (the grain still gives some resistance when bitten) remove from heat and stir in Parmesan cheese and butter. Cover and rest for 5 minutes off the heat, then serve immediately.

Presentation:

Spoon a helping of risotto in the centre of a large pasta bowl or soup plate. Place a lamb shank on top of the risotto and sprinkle with freshly chopped chives. Serve with your favourite vegetables: green beans or steamed broccoli are a good choice.

Serves 6

Braised Beef Brisket and Kidney Pie with Pickled Button Mushrooms

Steak and kidney pudding is a Sunday tradition in England, and this recipe was one I enjoyed on many weekends while working there years ago. It is equally popular in pubs, which are in many ways the "bistros" of England, the places where culturally important and locally inspired dishes are served. The British like it spicy and this sauce recipe is excellent if you like a big punch of flavour. It can be served as a stew without the crust — just add some carrots and potatoes to the recipe and enjoy it simply in a bowl. I love the caramelized edges of the crust so I rarely serve this any way but as described here. The pickled mushrooms are a nice side to this and make use of organic log-harvested button mushrooms available year-round in Nova Scotia and most Canadian provinces.

Pie Filling

3 lb (1.5 kg) beef brisket
1 large onion, diced
3 cloves garlic, minced
2 cups (500 mL) low-sodium beef broth (fresh is best)
1 cup (250 mL) red wine
¼ cup (60 mL) ketchup
½ cup (125 mL) Worcestershire sauce
½ cup (125 mL) HP Sauce
1 cup (250 mL) demi-glace
1 tbsp (15 mL) Tabasco sauce
1 tsp (5 mL) salt
1 lb (450 g) beef kidneys

Pie Dough

2 ½ cups (625 mL) unbleached white flour
1 tsp (5 mL) baking powder
½ tsp (3 mL) sea salt
1 cup (250 mL) frozen unsalted butter
½ to ¾ cup (125 to 180 mL) iced water
1 egg yolk
1 tsp (5 mL) white vinegar

Pickled Button Mushrooms

1 lb (450 g) whole button mushrooms
1 cup (250 mL) white wine vinegar
¼ cup (60 mL) water
1 tbsp (15 mL) sugar
1 small onion, halved
2 cloves garlic
6 whole black peppercorns
6 whole allspice
3 whole cloves
1 tsp (5 mL) pickling spice
½ tsp (3 mL) salt

For the filling:

Place all ingredients except beef kidneys in an ovenproof casserole dish and bake in a 325°F (165°C) oven for 3 hours. If you are using a powdered demi-glace, reconstitute it with water as directed on the package. When brisket is fork-tender, remove from the oven, place in a separate bowl until cool enough to handle, and flake meat with your fingers. You may have to cut meat into smaller pieces to do this easily. Bring sauce to a boil on the stove and reduce by one-third, or until slightly thickened.

Cut kidneys into small pieces (about 1 in / 2.5 cm). Mix kidneys and brisket back into sauce. Try to use a casserole dish sized such that meat and sauce come almost to the top.

For the dough:

Thoroughly combine flour, baking powder and salt in a mixing bowl. Remove butter from the freezer just before use and grate directly into the flour mixture using the large size of a box grater. In a separate bowl, mix iced water, egg yolk and vinegar together. Add to butter / flour mix and just bring together. Do not knead more than necessary. Wrap in plastic film and allow to rest for 90 minutes in refrigerator before using (overnight is best).

Roll out pie dough into a piece large enough to cover casserole dish. Brush top of dough with a little eggwash or cream. Trim edges if desired, but leave some over the dish to create lovely browned, crunchy pieces. Bake in a 350°F (180°C) oven for 35 to 40 minutes. Let stand for 10 minutes before serving. (Note: These pies can be made in small, individual ramekins as well, or as a turnover.)

Place a healthy portion of pie on a plate with a side serving of pickled mushrooms and your favourite simple vegetable or some mashed potato.

Serves 8

For the mushrooms:

Trim stems off mushrooms, leaving just the caps. Quickly rinse mushrooms under running water just before making the recipe, but not in advance. Bring all remaining ingredients to a boil and throw in mushrooms. Return to a boil and simmer for 5 minutes. Remove from the heat and rest until mushrooms reach room temperature. Remove onion halves and serve. The mushrooms can be kept refrigerated for several weeks or preserved using a standard jarring procedure.

Yields 4 cups (1 L)

Montreal Bacon Cheeseburger on a Brioche Bun

Paul McInnis, Tortoise and Hare General Store, Tantallon, Nova Scotia

Whether or not a burger recipe should find its way into any cookbook about Canadian bistro cooking could be debated, since it is a distinctly American invention and cultural food icon. Yet, as the foods of Italy, France and Great Britain have influenced our Canadian palate, surely the foods of our neighbours to the south have influenced it as much or more. Without a doubt, Chef Paul's burger recipe is the best I have ever eaten. The key is to make your own ground-beef patties using a meat grinder or food processor, and then to handle the patties as little as possible. Grinding the beef yourself means you can cook the burgers to a desired doneness without worrying about food-borne illness.

Burgers

2 lb (900 g) beef chuck, chilled
2 lb (900 g) boneless beef short ribs
2 tbsp (30 mL) Dijon mustard (hot dog mustard is fine)
2 tbsp (30 mL) your favorite barbecue sauce
2 tbsp (30 mL) Worcestershire sauce
2 tbsp (30 mL) soy sauce
2 tsp (10 mL) Montreal steak spice
8 slices smoked Gouda or Applewood cheddar cheese

Toppings

8 strips Montreal-style smoked bacon
1 lb (450 g) mixed wild mushrooms, roughly chopped
1 tbsp (15 mL) butter
¼ tsp (1 mL) salt
2 oz (60 g) mixed baby greens
2 large field tomatoes, sliced ¼ in (5 mm) thick

Brioche Buns

1 tbsp (15 mL) dry yeast
1 tbsp (15 mL) white sugar
⅓ cup plus 1 tbsp (100 mL) warm milk
2 cups (500 mL) unbleached white flour
½ tsp (3 mL) salt
¼ tsp (1 mL) finely ground black pepper
⅓ cup (85 mL) softened butter
2 free-range eggs, at room temperature
1 egg yolk (for eggwash)
1 tsp (5 mL) milk
1 tbsp (15 mL) sesame seeds
½ tsp (3 mL) rock salt

For the burgers:

Chill beef until it is as cold as possible, almost frozen. Cut the two types of beef into approximately 1-in (2.5-cm) cubes. In a food processor, pulse chuck and ribs until they are in small pieces but not over-processed and pasty. If you have a grinding attachment to your stand mixer you can use it instead. Mix beef, mustard, sauces and steak spice gently with your fingers until just combined, and form into 8 x 8-oz (225-g) patties. Handle burgers as little as possible and keep them very cold.

Preheat and clean the grill of your barbecue thoroughly, and sear patties over high heat. After two minutes, rotate them 90 degrees, without flipping. Grill 2 minutes more, flip and repeat. Place burgers on the top rack of your barbecue and reduce the flame to medium, to finish cooking at a lower temperature. (The burgers will retain more moisture as they cook. Also, if left too long on the bottom grill, the fat content will cause flare-ups.) While burgers finish on the top rack, toast Brioche Buns on the lower rack.

Cook burgers until desired doneness is reached. Don't be afraid to peek inside and check the colour of the meat and juices. Clear juices indicate that the burger is done. If you use a thermometer, it should reach 150°F (65°C) for medium and 180°F (85°C) for well done (if using pre-ground beef). Place a piece of smoked cheese on each burger and allow to melt.

For the toppings:

Lay bacon on a baking tray and bake in a 350°F (180°C) oven for 12 minutes. Remove and pat dry with a clean paper towel to remove any excess fat. Hold in a warm oven or simply grill for 60 seconds on the barbecue before assembling burgers.

Sauté mushrooms in butter and salt until slightly caramelized. This should take about 10 minutes over medium high heat. Reserve warm until burgers are ready. Assemble burgers and garnish as you would typically enjoy them, adding some of the greens and sliced tomato. Suggested toppings are mustard and mayo. Ketchup is not the best condiment for this burger as it masks the great smoked flavour of the bacon and cheese. Raw white onions are a must.

Yields 8 burgers

For the brioche buns:

In the bottom of an electric mixing bowl, combine dry yeast, sugar and milk. Let sit for 5 minutes until it just begins to froth.

Sift together flour, salt and pepper and add to milk. Using the hook attachment of your mixer, combine on low speed until a batter forms. Continue mixing and add softened butter to dough, about 1 tbsp (15 mL) at a time. Then add eggs one at a time until they too are fully incorporated into dough.

Rest dough, covered, in a warm place until it doubles in size, then push it down and knead again with the hook attachment for another 5 to 10 minutes. Cut dough into 8 equal-sized pieces and form into rounds. Place on a greased baking sheet (or one lined with non-stick parchment paper) and allow to rise again for about 1 hour.

When buns have doubled in size, brush with an eggwash of beaten egg yolk and 1 tsp (5 mL) of milk. Sprinkle with sesame seeds and rock salt. Bake in a 400°F (200°C) oven until golden brown on the bottoms and tops (about 12 minutes, depending on oven).

Yields 8 buns

Herb-stuffed Chicken with Wholegrain Polenta and Sautéed Chanterelle Mushrooms

Rémi Cousyn, Calories, Saskatoon, Saskatchewan

Rémi Cousyn grew up in Provence, France. With blood like that in his veins he was born to cook. I had the privilege of working with Rémi in 2008 at Michael Stadlander's inaugural Canadian Chefs' Congress. My memory of Rémi is standing next to each other for 8 hours prepping dishes for 500 hungry guests. He was boning quail and I was shelling lobster (cooks have a way of bonding during periods of great suffering). Rémi, like so many chefs in this country, takes a regional and seasonal approach to food and tries to showcase simple flavours. In this dish, everything is geared towards letting the chicken taste like chicken and the chanterelles come to the forefront. It is beautiful food and healthy, even with the cream — a true Canadian bistro dish.

Herb-stuffed Chicken

8 free-range chicken breasts (skin on, wing bone in)
1 sprig fresh thyme, finely chopped
4 leaves fresh sage, finely chopped
¼ cup (60 mL) grated Parmesan cheese
1 tsp (5 mL) salt
½ tsp (3 mL) freshly ground black pepper
⅓ cup (85 mL) 35% cream
2 tbsp (30 mL) chopped parsley
2 tbsp (30 mL) chopped chives
3 tbsp (45 mL) olive oil
3 tbsp (45 mL) butter

Wholegrain Polenta

3 oz (80 g) wild rice
4 cups (1 L) milk
1 bay leaf
1 tsp (5 mL) salt
½ tsp (3 mL) black pepper
3 oz (80 g) cornmeal
1 ½ oz (40 g) cracked wheat
3 oz (80 g) rolled oats
3 oz (80 g) ground flax
4 tbsp (60 mL) butter
½ cup (125 mL) grated Parmesan cheese

Sautéed Chanterelle Mushrooms

3 ½ oz (100 g) shallots, finely sliced
1 clove garlic, minced
3 oz (80 g) butter
2 to 2 ½ lb (900 to 1350 g) fresh chanterelles, washed and trimmed
1 tsp (5 mL) salt
1 tsp (5 mL) freshly ground black pepper
1 sprig fresh thyme, leaves picked
½ cup (125 mL) dry white wine
1 cup (250 mL) 35% cream

For the chicken:

Remove chicken tenders (the small attached pieces of meat on the underside of each breast) from each supreme. Use a small knife to cut away the silver tendon in each and place meat in a food processor. Add thyme, sage, Parmesan, salt, and pepper and process on high. Rapidly add cream through the top hatch of the food processor until a smooth mousseline forms. Fold in parsley and chives with a spatula (this will prevent the mousseline from turning green). Place filling in a piping bag and refrigerate until ready for use.

Using a small paring or boning knife, cut a pocket in the middle of each chicken breast, just under the wing bone (where the meat is thickest). You can use your finger to widen the pocket but try not to puncture or tear the meat. Pipe filling equally into breasts.

Season chicken on both sides with salt and pepper. Heat a skillet on high and sear breasts in oil, skin side down, until caramelized and golden brown. Add butter to pan and place in a 400°F (200°C) oven for 6 minutes. Remove from the oven and flip chicken, then reduce the heat to 300°F (150°C), return to the oven and cook for about 6 to 8 more minutes. Rest for at least 10 minutes before slicing and serving with polenta and chanterelles.

For the polenta:

Cook wild rice in lightly salted water for 40 minutes, or until tender. Bring milk to a boil with bay leaf, salt and pepper. Remove bay leaf. Slowly add cornmeal, cracked wheat and rolled oats to milk. Whisk gently for 15 to 20 minutes. Fold in flax, cooked rice, butter and Parmesan cheese. Adjust seasoning.

For the mushrooms:

Sauté shallots and garlic in butter for a minute or two. Add chanterelles, salt and pepper and sauté until their water has evaporated. Remove chanterelles from the pan and set aside. Add thyme, deglaze pan with white wine and reduce until almost all liquid has evaporated. Add any juices from the chicken. Add cream and cook until sauce has reduced and slightly thickened. Return chanterelles to cream sauce, adjust seasoning and serve.

Presentation:

Spoon a helping of polenta onto a warm plate. Slice chicken breast into 2 or 3 pieces and place on top of polenta, then spoon chanterelles in cream over the top.

Serves 8

Barbecued Pork Roast with Fruit Chutney Glaze

Mark Gabrieau, Gabrieau's Bistro, Antigonish, Nova Scotia

If you are looking for an alternative way to barbecue, this is the dish for you. The fruit chutney is incredibly versatile and can be jarred for the winter. It has a sweet-and-sour flavour that goes well with a hundred different meats or poultry recipes, but with this shoulder or butt roast it especially shines, probably because it is inspired by the apple sauce traditionally served with Sunday pork. It requires a low and slow heat that reserves the precious moisture within the meat. With each swipe of the pastry brush, the fruit glaze gets stickier and more delicious.

Pork

3 cups (750 mL) low-sodium chicken stock (fresh or canned)
1 tsp (15 mL) pickling or kosher salt
1 cup (250 mL) liquid honey
¼ cup (60 mL) brown sugar
2 tbsp (30 mL) crushed black peppercorns
3 tbsp (45 mL) crushed dried rosemary
¾ cup (180 mL) crushed garlic cloves
1 large onion, diced
1 bay leaf
1 tbsp (15 mL) mustard seeds
½ tsp (3 mL) freshly grated nutmeg
1 pod star anise
1 x 5-lb (2.5-kg) pork shoulder or butt roast
1 cup (250 mL) Fruit Chutney Glaze (recipe follows)

Fruit Chutney Glaze

1 tsp (5 mL) whole allspice
1 tsp (5 mL) whole cloves
2 cups (500 mL) sliced mixed peaches, apples or pears (use what you have)
1 cup (250 mL) sliced fresh apricots
2 cups (500 mL) mandarin oranges
1 cup (250 mL) melon
2 ¼ cups (560 mL) sugar
1 ½ cups (375 mL) apple cider vinegar
1 cinnamon stick
juice and zest of 2 oranges
1 cup (250 mL) currants
1 shallot, diced

For the pork:

In a pot, place all ingredients *except* pork and Fruit Chutney Glaze, and bring to a boil. Let cool and pour over pork. Marinate for 2 to 4 days. On the day you wish to serve pork, remove from marinade and pat dry with paper towels. Refrigerate until ready for the grill.

Preheat barbecue to high. Grill pork on lower rack of grill or barbecue. When flesh is slightly charred and caramelized, coat with Fruit Chutney Glaze and move roast to the upper rack. Turn heat dial to low or medium-low (depending on the intensity of your barbecue) and lower the cover. Bake until the internal temperature is approximately 160°F (70°C), basting with fruit chutney every ten minutes or so. Let rest for a minimum of 30 minutes before carving.

This roast can be served like any family roast dinner, with potatoes, a green salad or another barbecued side dish like corn on the cob or grilled vegetables.

Serves 8 to 10

For the glaze:

Place allspice and cloves in a piece of cheesecloth and tie with a string for easy removal later. Place all ingredients in a large pot and bring to a boil, stirring occasionally. Reduce heat and cook for about 1 hour, or until darkened and slightly thickened. Let cool and remove cheesecloth sachet and cinnamon stick, then purée in a food processor to the consistency of jam or jelly. If it seems watery or too loose after puréeing, it can be returned to the stove and reduced to the correct consistency. Place in jars and refrigerate.

Yields 6 cups, or 3 x 500 mL Mason jars

Braised Heritage Pork Shoulder with Blackberry Jam Sauce

Michael Howell, Tempest Restaurant, Wolfville, Nova Scotia

Michael's use of heritage pork has increased the profile of this delicious and underutilized meat in our Canadian food culture. Many heritage pork varieties are being produced on small farms all over the country: Tamworth, Large Black, Berkshire and Yorkshire to name just a few. As you can tell by the names, these breeds were originally domesticated in the U.K. The biggest difference with heritage meat is in the colour, fat content and earthy flavour. Michael's recipe below is wonderfully versatile. It can be served as a Sunday roast or fork-pulled and served on a toasted bun. The sauce is sweet and delicious and makes use of the summer's berry harvest with a new and tasty approach.

1 quart (1 L) fresh blackberries

2 cups (500 mL) pulp-free orange juice

½ cup (125 mL) lemon juice

4 large bay leaves, lightly crushed

1 tsp (5 mL) ground cumin

1 small bunch fresh thyme sprigs

1 tsp (5 mL) peppercorns

¼ cup (60 mL) extra-virgin olive oil

1 tbsp (15 mL) white sugar

1 cup (250 mL) chicken or (preferably) pork stock

1 x 3-lb (1.5-kg) Heritage pork shoulder (such as Tamworth or Berkshire), bone in

3 tbsp (45 mL) blackberry jam

1 tsp (5 mL) cornstarch

¼ cup (60 mL) water (or stock, if desired)

In a small mixing bowl, combine blackberries, orange juice, lemon juice, bay leaves, cumin, thyme sprigs, peppercorns, olive oil and sugar. Combine well. Put in an airtight plastic bag and add pork shoulder. Swish pork around to completely coat, seal bag with a twist tie, put in a bowl or container and refrigerate for a minimum of 4 hours and up to 48 hours.

Three hours before serving, preheat oven to 325°F (165°C). Remove pork from the bag, place in a roasting pan with marinade, cover tightly and roast for 3 hours. Remove lid, flip pork over and raise temperature to 375°F (190°C). Add blackberry jam to marinade. Roast for an additional 20 to 30 minutes, then remove from oven.

Carefully remove any accumulated juices to a defatting cup (a regular large measuring cup works too). Let sit for 15 minutes (while pork is resting) and remove excess fat from the top. Return sauce to the stove in a small saucepan, bring to a boil, and stir in cornstarch that has been dissolved in water or stock. Cook over medium-high heat until thickened.

With two forks, break pork apart into small bite-sized pieces. Serve with sauce poured over the top and with roasted apples, parsnips and Brussels sprouts. It can also be served in a toasted roll as a sandwich.

Serves 6 to 8

Pine Mushroom Scented Chicken

Michael Allemeier, Mission Hill Winery, Okanagan Valley, British Columbia

I had the great pleasure of cooking for three days with Michael at Mission Hill Winery in 2004. Michael is wonderful at understanding how to make wine shine next to his food. The wines of Mission Hill are as important in his cooking as his ingredients. Michael is a family man and this simple roast chicken dish is a perfect family Sunday supper that kids will enjoy. "This recipe was made when I was living in Whistler, B.C." he recalls. "That fall was a bumper year for pine mushrooms, or *Matsutake* as the Japanese know them. This mushroom is pure white, with firm, dense flesh — the aroma of the mushrooms permeates the chicken as it roasts."

1 x 5-lb (2.2-kg) free-range chicken
2 tbsp (30 mL) coarse sea salt
1 large onion, diced
¾ lb (330 g) butter
4 slices day-old sourdough bread, diced
5 leaves fresh sage, chopped
1 lb (450 g) fresh pine mushrooms

Wash chicken well with cold water and pat dry. Season inside and out with ½ of the salt. Cook onion in butter over medium heat until softened, about 5 minutes. Place in a mixing bowl and add diced bread and sage leaves. Brush off any dirt from mushrooms, slice, mix with bread and season with remaining salt. Stuff chicken with bread and mushroom stuffing.

Preheat oven to 350°F (180°C). Place chicken on a roasting tray and cover with remaining butter. Roast until cooked (about 20 minutes per pound, 40 minutes per kg), then let rest in a warm place for at least 30 minutes before serving. Remove stuffing and serve alongside the carved roast chicken.

Serves 4

Roast Canada Goose with Brandy Marmalade Sauce

Ray Lovell, Combat Catering, Iqaluit, Nunavut

Whether or not you like Canada goose, there could hardly be a better single ingredient to unite the chefs of our country. Ray Lovell has cooked with the goose in his region for many years and enjoys the gamey flavour in the meat. Such a recipe could become a classic Canadian Christmas or Thanksgiving entree, especially given the number of geese that we see just before their return south. But if you are hesitant to try the wild variety, a farm-raised goose is just fine too. The citrus notes remind one of a classic French bistro *Duck a l'Orange.*

1 x 7- to 8-lb (3- to 3.5-kg) Canada goose (young)

1 tbsp (15 mL) salt

1 tbsp (15 mL) freshly ground black pepper

1 white of leek, thinly sliced and washed

2 medium onions, diced

2 stalks celery, chopped

1 orange, peeled, segmented and chopped

2 apples, peeled and diced small

½ cup (125 mL) finely chopped double-smoked bacon

2 tbsp (30 mL) fresh thyme leaves

2 tbsp (30 mL) chopped fresh sage

2 tbsp (30 mL) chopped fresh rosemary

2 carrots, coarsely chopped

¼ cup (60 mL) Worcestershire sauce

1 small jar orange or citrus marmalade

1 small jar apricot jam

½ cup (125 mL) brandy

Wash goose under cold running water and pat dry with paper towels. Season inside and out with salt and freshly ground black pepper. Preheat oven to 350°F (180°C).

In a large mixing bowl combine sliced leek, one diced onion, one chopped celery stalk, orange, apples, bacon and chopped fresh herbs. Tie bird closed with a trussing needle or a piece of butcher's twine. In a roasting pan make a bed of the second chopped onion, celery stalk and carrots.

Place goose on bed of vegetables and douse with Worcestershire sauce. Pour in just enough cold water to cover vegetables (use chicken stock for extra flavour) and place in oven. Baste bird every 45 minutes to prevent it from getting too dry and to help maintain that perfect golden brown colour. The goose is perfectly cooked when the leg bone can be gripped, pulled, and comes out cleanly with clear juices. A bird will take 4 to 5 hours to cook, depending on your oven (convection ovens will take less time even at the same temperature). Rest goose for at least 30 minutes, tented under aluminum foil, before carving.

Mix marmalade and jam in a saucepan with brandy. Flambé brandy and burn off the alcohol, then whisk to a saucelike consistency. Add some water if needed.

Serve this simple sauce with roast goose and your favourite fixings, like mashed potatoes and roasted root vegetables.

Serves 8 to 10

Canned Moose Tagliatelle

The inspiration for this dish came from an apprentice whose family preserves moose meat in New Brunswick each year. This is even more of a tradition in Newfoundland. On a trip to Piedmont, Italy, I fell in love with the famous regional bistro dish of rabbit ragout and handmade tajarin pasta called "*tajarin al sugo di lepre*." Back home, the succulent and gamey moose meat replaces the hare in this hearty and delicious recipe and creates a very distinctive meat sauce. I call this a spring recipe because it makes use of the season's first greenhouse tomatoes, but you can make it year round. This dish is a real cross-cultural experiment, but it works. Simple and delicious, if you have canned or preserved moose in your larder, crack a bottle of Barolo and make it an Italian night.

1 onion, minced

1 carrot, grated

2 cloves garlic, minced

1 tbsp (15 mL) olive oil

1 tbsp (15 mL) butter

1 tsp (5 mL) salt

1 tsp (5 mL) freshly ground black pepper

½ tsp (3 mL) dried chili flakes

2 tbsp (30 mL) tomato paste

1 cup (250 mL) red wine

1 large can (12-to 16-oz/375-to 500-mL) crushed Italian tomatoes

3 cups (750 mL) diced fresh greenhouse tomatoes

1 jar or can (16-oz/500 mL) cooked moose meat

1 box dried tagliatelle noodles

½ cup (125 mL) 35% cream

¼ cup (60 mL) sliced ("chiffonade") fresh basil leaves

½ cup (125 mL) Parmesan cheese

3 tbsp (45 mL) chopped fresh flatleaf Italian parsley

Sauté onion, carrot and garlic in olive oil and butter and season immediately with salt, pepper and chili flakes. Cook until vegetables are translucent and soft, about 5 minutes. Add tomato paste and cook for 5 more minutes. Deglaze pan with red wine and reduce by half. Add tomatoes and moose meat and bring to a simmer. Cook for at least 1 hour on low heat, until sauce is slightly thickened and moose meat is tender and falls apart.

Prepare tagliatelle noodles according to the instructions on the box. Use salted water and plenty of it to cook pasta properly. It should take no more than 7 minutes if the water is boiling. Strain pasta and return to the pasta pot. Add one 8-oz (225-mL) ladle of sauce and stir well. Portion pasta into bowls.

Add cream and basil leaves to the rest of the sauce and bring just to the boil. Stir in cheese and ladle a generous portion of sauce over pasta in each bowl. Garnish with extra Parmesan cheese and parsley.

Serves 6 to 8

Red Thai Curried Caribou

Ray Lovell, Combat Catering, Iqaluit, Nunavut

Reindeer, or caribou, has been hunted for centuries in Northern countries like Canada and Scandinavia. Declining woodland caribou populations in this country have resulted in Newfoundland being the only province where legal hunting is still allowed. However, with the ever-more-knowledgeable consumer desiring a more interesting selection of proteins, farm-raised caribou/reindeer has become more popular. I can guarantee there are no caribou in Thailand, so in this recipe Chef Lovell has definitely created a cross-cultural dish. It is actually a perfect way to serve the rich and slightly gamey meat, with some warmth and spice. Ray suggests serving it with your favorite rice such as jasmine or basmati in a simple pilaf.

1x1 ½-lb (675-g) boneless leg of caribou
salt and cracked pepper to taste
3 tbsp (45 mL) olive oil or vegetable oil
2 medium-sized onions, thinly sliced
3 cloves garlic, minced
2 tbsp (30 mL) red Thai curry paste
1 tbsp (15 mL) demerara sugar
12 kaffir lime leaves
⅓ cup (85 mL) caribou, game or beef stock
1 cup (250 mL) good quality coconut milk
2 medium-sized red bell peppers, julienned
juice of 2 kaffir limes
24 whole water chestnuts
2 tsp (10 mL) fish sauce
fresh chopped cilantro, for garnish
Thai basil, for garnish

Trim caribou meat of any bone fragments and cut into 1 ½-in (4-cm) pieces. Season with a little salt and pepper. In a large cast iron skillet, heat oil until it begins to smoke. Add seasoned caribou, onions and garlic and cook until a nice caramel colour appears.

Add red Thai curry paste, sugar and kaffir lime leaves, and cook for a few minutes over medium heat. Cover meat with stock and coconut milk and bring stew to a roiling boil. Reduce the heat and add red bell peppers and lime juice, cover with a lid and place in a 300°F (150°C) oven for about 1 hour, or until caribou is fork-tender.

Remove from the oven and add water chestnuts and fish sauce. Adjust seasoning as desired. Garnish with the chopped cilantro and a chiffonade of Thai basil and Thai basil sprigs.

Serves 4 to 6

Beef Cheeks à la Souvavou with Celery Root, Apple and Potato Purée

Anthony Walsh, Canoe and Biff's Bistro, Toronto, Ontario

You probably won't find beef cheeks in your grocery store, but an independent butcher can get you some. They are feared by many, more for the idea of what they are than for the flavour. Bistros and small family-run restaurants all over Europe make use of every cut of the animal. Many of the greatest dishes in the world come from using scraps or leftovers: osso bucco, beef Bourguignon, lobster bisque, sausages from all over the world, pâtés and terrines, and even the pub favourite potato skins! Anthony serves this dish with small baby beets in the summer and some roasted root vegetables in the winter. This dish is absolutely wonderful and is worth any extra effort.

Beef Cheeks

4 large beef cheeks, halved
1 bottle (750 mL) medium-bodied red wine (Merlot or
    Cabernet Sauvignon)
½ cup (125 mL) chopped onion
1 medium cup (125 mL) carrot, cut into 1-in (2.5-cm) pieces
½ cup (125 mL) chopped white of leek
3 cloves garlic, smashed
2 sprigs thyme
2 bay leaves
8 juniper berries
1 tsp (5 mL) crushed black peppercorns
16 bacon lardons, cut small
16 cloves roasted garlic
salt and pepper
flour for dusting
4 tbsp (60 mL) olive oil
2 cups (500 mL) good veal or beef stock
3 tbsp (45 mL) cold butter (to finish sauce after braising)

Dough

1 cup (250 mL) flour
½ cup (125 mL) cold water

Celery Root, Apple and Potato Purée

1 lb (450 g) celery root, peeled and coarsely chopped
3 cups (750 mL) milk
1 bay leaf
1 sprig fresh thyme
2 tart apples, peeled and chopped
1 lb (450 g) Yukon Gold potatoes, peeled and diced
6 tbsp (90 mL) 35% cream
1 tsp (5 mL) ground nutmeg
2 tbsp (30 mL) butter
1 tsp (5 mL) salt
freshly ground black pepper

For the beef cheeks:

Trim exterior gristle from beef cheeks but leave the silver skin that runs through the middle (this will cook very tender). Marinate beef cheeks overnight in the refrigerator with wine, onion, carrot, leek, garlic, herbs and spices. Remove cheeks and set aside. Strain vegetables from wine and reserve, and in a small saucepan, bring wine to a boil for 3 minutes. Strain through cheesecloth or fine-meshed chinois and reserve.

Using a boning or paring knife, cut 4 tiny pockets in each cheek and stuff with bacon and half a roasted garlic clove. (Note: whole roasted garlic can be made by roasting an entire head of garlic and carefully peeling the paper from each clove once it has cooled.) Tie each cheek using butcher's twine "parcel style," season liberally with salt and pepper and dredge in flour. Heat a large casserole dish (one with a properly fitted lid) over medium-high heat and brown cheeks in olive oil until golden brown. Remove cheeks from the casserole and add reserved vegetables and spices, lightly browning them for about 5 minutes. Add reserved wine to deglaze the casserole. Reduce wine by half and add stock and beef cheeks. Bring to a simmer.

For the dough:

Mix flour and water together and roll out into a "snake," then press dough onto the inside of the casserole lid. Place the lid on the top of the dish of simmering cheeks and form a tight seal. Place cheeks in a 350°F (180°C) oven and braise for 3 hours.

When cheeks are ready, allow them to cool in braising liquid. This lets them hydrate after cooking. Remove cheeks and strain vegetables from braising liquid. In a saucepan, reduce liquid by half. Check seasonings of reduction and add salt and pepper if desired.

For the purée:

In a saucepan, cook celery root, milk, bay leaf and thyme for 10 to 15 minutes, covered with a lid or cartouche (a piece of parchment paper cut to fit into the pan and sit on top of the liquid). Add apples and cook for a further 10 minutes, until both apples and celery root are fork-tender. In a blender, process mixture until velvety smooth.

In a separate pot, cook potatoes in salted water until tender. Process potatoes through a tamis, food mill or potato ricer to avoid lumps.

Add celery root mixture to potatoes and whisk in warmed 35% cream, nutmeg and butter. Adjust salt and pepper if needed and serve immediately.

Presentation:

Snip strings from each cheek and place one per person in the centre of a pile of Parsley Root, Apple and Potato Purée. Reheat sauce and whisk in cold butter just before serving. Spoon some of the rich sauce over each cheek and garnish with your favourite vegetables.

Serves 8

Shepherd's Pie

I always enjoyed shepherd's pie as a child, but even more so when I was travelling throughout the U.K., where it is often featured on pub menus. Of course, "shepherd's pie" contains lamb and "cottage pie" uses beef, though on our continent ground beef is usually the favourite choice. I prefer to serve the vegetables on the side, but you can add some peas, carrots or corn if you wish. It can either be made in a single casserole dish or individual dishes. The idea here is to worry less about looks and more about taste. This is simple rustic bistro food, and I doubt if you have ever had a tastier version.

Filling

1 x 2-lb (900-g) boneless lamb shoulder
3 tbsp (45 mL) olive oil
1 medium onion, diced
1 carrot, diced
1 stalk celery, diced
2 cups (500 mL) beef or lamb broth
2 cups (500 mL) red wine
2 bay leaves
4 fresh mint stalks

Aged Cheddar Potato Purée

2 lb (900 g) unpeeled potatoes
1 cup (250 mL) milk
½ cup (125 mL) 35% cream
½ lb (225 g) salted butter
1 tsp (5 mL) sea salt
1 tsp (5 mL) freshly ground black pepper
1 tsp (5 mL) grated fresh nutmeg
1 cup (250 mL) grated aged white Canadian cheddar
½ cup (125 mL) corn or frozen sweet peas (optional)

For the filling:

In a large stainless steel pot or brazier sear lamb in olive oil until browned on all sides. Remove and rest on a separate plate. Place onion, carrot and celery in the pot and then rest lamb on top. Add beef or lamb broth, red wine, bay leaves and mint stalks. Bring pot just to a boil and place, covered, in a 300°F (150°C) oven for 2 to 2 ½ hours, or until meat is flaky and very tender. Let meat cool in braising liquid for at least 1 hour.

When meat is cool enough to handle, remove it from braising liquid and strain through a sieve into a clean saucepan. Discard vegetables and herbs and bring the liquid to a boil. Reduce by half, or until it coats the back of a spoon. You can also thicken sauce with a little cornstarch if desired.

While sauce is reducing, pull meat apart, using 2 forks or your fingertips, into small shreds or bite-sized pieces. Then add sauce to meat and mix well. Adjust seasonings if needed and refrigerate until you are ready to assemble pies.

For the potato purée:

Cook potatoes in salted water until fork-tender. Remove from water and, using a towel to protect your hands, peel potatoes while hot. Mill or rice potatoes into a bowl or stockpot. Heat milk, cream, butter, salt, pepper and nutmeg in a small saucepan. Pour into milled potatoes and beat quickly with a whisk. Add cheese and adjust seasoning if necessary with a little sea salt.

To assemble:

If using individual ramekins or lasagna dishes, approximately 10 oz (300 mL) in volume, or a large casserole dish, fill the bottom half with pulled lamb shoulder meat. Pat meat down using the back of a spoon or your fingers. Add a tablespoon per serving of corn or frozen sweet peas at this point if you wish, otherwise begin spooning potato onto meat. Using the back of a spoon or a long metal spatula spread potato purée evenly over the top of each dish, so it is flat and smooth. For a more traditional look, pipe potato on top.

Bake pies in a preheated 350°F (180°C) oven until slightly browned on top and hot all the way through, about 20 to 30 minutes, depending on the size.

Serve pies with a simple salad, some steamed peas and carrots, or on their own.

Serves 6 to 8

Fink's Beef Brisket with Sweet Potato Latkes

Paul Finkelstein, Screaming Avocado Café, Stratford, Ontario

Paul Finkelstein's incredible talent for teaching, sense of humour, boundless energy and creativity with food have made him one of Canada's most recognizable chefs. I have travelled to Europe twice with Paul, as he shares my passion and interest in the Slow Food movement in this country and around the world. One of Slow Food's goals is to protect and savour old recipes, teach people how to cook them and reintroduce them into a fast-paced, modern world. Paul does this here, as his Jewish heritage is extremely important to him and several of his favourite dishes, like this one, respect the old traditions he grew up with.

Beef Brisket

1 ½ cups (375 mL) diced tomatoes (fresh or canned)
½ cup (125 mL) ketchup
2 cups (500 mL) beef stock
¼ cup (60 mL) packed brown sugar
½ cup (125 mL) molasses
2 cups (500 mL) red wine
2 onions, sliced
1 head garlic, cut in half
2 sprigs thyme
1 bay leaf
4 lb (2 kg) beef brisket
1 tsp (5 mL) salt
2 carrots, peeled and coarsely chopped

Sweet Potato Latkes (Pancakes)

2 large sweet potatoes
1/2 onion, coarsely grated
1 egg
4 sprigs thyme, leaves picked
½ cup (125 mL) flour
1 tsp (5 mL) salt
½ tsp (3 mL) pepper
1 cup (250 mL) olive and vegetable oil blend
   (approximately)
sour cream and chives (optional), for garnish

For the beef:

In a bowl, mix tomatoes, ketchup, beef stock, sugar, molasses and wine. Set aside. Toss onions, garlic, thyme and bay leaf in a roasting pan and place brisket on top, fat side up. Sprinkle with salt. Pour tomato mixture over and around brisket. Cover tightly with aluminum foil, as steam will keep meat moist and help to tenderize it.

Cook in a preheated 350°F (180°C) for 1 ½ hours. Add carrots, reseal and return to the oven until tender, approximately 3 hours. Remove from the oven and rest in braising liquid for 1 hour. Remove and slice brisket across long grain of meat (this will make brisket more tender and palatable). Strain sauce, squeezing out garlic cloves first. Place sauce back on the stove and reduce by half, or until a nice loose sauce forms. This sauce can be used to glaze the meat just before serving.

For the latkes:

Wash sweet potatoes. If skins are clean, keep them on, otherwise peel them. Grate potatoes and onion into a bowl, and add egg, thyme leaves, flour, salt and pepper and mix well.

Heat ¼ in (5 mm) of oil in a skillet over medium-high heat until quite hot. Using a large spoon, carefully place batter into skillet in roughly 3-in (7.5-cm) diameter circles, and use a spatula to flatten them out. Try to keep them the same size for cooking time and presentation. Fry to golden brown on both sides, 3 to 4 minutes per side, adjusting the heat accordingly. Don't fry more than three or four at a time as they will take longer to cook and won't crisp up nicely. Drain on paper towels.

Serve latkes with the beef brisket and some steamed vegetables (broccoli goes well). Garnish with a little sour cream and chives if desired.

Serves 8

Cassoulet

Rob Fracchioni, The Millcroft Inn & Spa, Alton-Caledon, Ontario

Cassoulet is one of the oldest and simplest peasant dishes, originating in the south of France. Basically, it consists of meat and beans. Whenever I taste cassoulet I think of Saturday night supper as a kid. Memories of a mother's cooking is likely what endears this dish to so many. This dish has to be the ultimate comfort food dish for anyone with French heritage. Rob's version is quite traditional, with one unique and, I think, brilliant adjustment. I have often found that the beans make a cassoulet a touch flat. Rob adds some maple syrup, orange zest and good balsamic vinegar for acidity and balance that works very well with the meatiness of the dish. Choose whatever locally made sausages you can find.

1 lb (450 g) double-smoked bacon, diced

2 cups (500mL) finely chopped onion

1 cup (250 mL) finely chopped celery

1 cup (250 mL) carrot, in ⅛-in (3-mm) dice

1 lb (450 g) white beans

½ lb (225 g) dried green flageolet beans

1 smoked ham hock

4 bay leaves

1 bunch fresh thyme, leaves picked

4 leaves fresh sage, chopped

8 cups (2 L) chicken stock

2 pieces confit duck legs

1 lb (450 g) Kielbasa sausage, in ¼-in (5-mm) dice

1 lb (450 g) hot, locally made sausage, in ¼-in (5-mm) dice

¼ cup (60 mL) maple syrup

juice and zest of 1 orange

¼ cup (60 mL) good balsamic vinegar

salt and pepper to taste

In a large pot, over very low heat, slowly cook bacon until rendered and golden brown. Add onion, celery and carrot and cook until carrot is soft. Add beans, ham hock, bay leaves, thyme, sage and stock and simmer for 1 hour. Remove ham hock and pick all meat into little pieces, discarding bone. Return meat to the pot and add remaining ingredients. Simmer until beans are soft, about 2 hours. Remove bones from the duck legs before serving.

Season with salt and pepper to taste, depending on spiciness of sausage used.

Serves 10 to 12

Cornish Pastry with Beet Chutney

Ross and Simon Fraser, Fraser Café, Ottawa, Ontario

The Fraser brothers have opened their dream restaurant in a neighborhood near the Byward Market in Ottawa. It has created a buzz for its incredibly flavourful and unique versions of classic dishes. This version of the Cornish Pastry is a great year-round recipe as it uses those cold-stored items that we Canadian chefs rely on before the growing season erupts, as well as fresh ingredients when available. "Pastry-wrapped meat" is found in nearly every culture in one form or another, but this one pays homage to a British influence in our mainstream diet. The brothers also recommend trying the filling with duck confit, pulled pork or the traditional beef. This is classic cool-weather food.

Pastry

2 ½ cups (375 mL) flour
1 tsp (5 mL) salt
1 tbsp (15 mL) sugar
½ lb (225 g) cold butter, cubed
¼ to ½ cup (60 to 125 mL) iced water

Filling

1 small onion, minced
2 carrots, finely diced
2 stalks celery, finely chopped
4 cloves garlic, minced
¼ cup (60 mL) butter
1 tsp (5 mL) salt
1 tsp (5 mL) freshly ground pepper
½ cup (125 mL) white wine
1 Yukon Gold potato, peeled and finely diced
½ cup (125 mL) chicken stock
2 cups (500 mL) 35% cream
3 tbsp (45 mL) finely chopped fresh herbs, such as parsley,
    tarragon and thyme
½ roasted whole chicken, pulled and roughly chopped
    (about 1 lb / 450 g of meat)
2 tbsp (30 mL) grainy mustard
2 tbsp (30 mL) apple cider vinegar
1 egg, beaten (for eggwash)

Beet Chutney

6 red beets, peeled and diced
3 apples, peeled and diced
1 large white onion, diced
4 cups (1 L) white vinegar
3 cups (750 mL) sugar
3 tbsp (45 mL) grated fresh ginger
2 tbsp (30 mL) mustard seeds

For the pastry:

In a food processor combine flour, salt, sugar and butter. Pulse the machine until the mixture resembles coarse meal. Add ¼ cup (60 mL) of cold water and process again until dough just holds together when pinched. Add remaining water if necessary. Be sure not to overwork. Remove from the processor bowl and pat into a ball, wrap in plastic film and refrigerate for at least 30 minutes.

For the filling:

In a pot, sweat onion, carrots, celery and garlic with butter for approximately 5 minutes, season with salt and pepper and deglaze with white wine. Add potato, stock, cream and herbs and cook for about 10 to 15 minutes, until reduced and potatoes are cooked. Add chicken, mustard and vinegar and bring to a boil, then remove from the heat. The mixture should be stiff, not soupy or showing any signs of excess liquid. If it does, cook a little longer, uncovered, to evaporate more liquid.

On a lightly floured surface roll out dough to ¼-in (5-mm) thickness and cut 12 x 5-in (13-cm) diameter circles.

Fill each pie circle with roughly 2 oz (60g) of the mixture, brush half the edge of the pastry with eggwash and fold to make a turnover. Press tightly to create a good seal. Crimp the closed edge with a fork. Place on a baking sheet lined with parchment paper. Brush pastries with eggwash and bake at 375°F (190°C) for 15 minutes, until golden brown.

Serve pastries warm from the oven, two per person, with a side serving of Beet Chutney. Garnish with baby lettuce leaves or a simple side green salad.

Serves 6

For the beet chutney:

Combine all ingredients in a pot and cook at a low simmer for 30 to 45 minutes, until beets are tender. The chutney can be jarred and preserved if desired.

Yields 8 cups (2 L)

Steak Frites (Grilled Flatiron Steak with Peppercorn Cream Sauce and Crispy Pommes Frites)

Steak frites could be the ultimate bistro dish, at least in France or New York. I believe the Canadian version should feature great grass-fed or Alberta beef, late-summer yellow-fleshed potatoes and a tangy peppercorn sauce inspired by another beef favorite, *steak Diane*. Flatiron steak is cut from the shoulder of the animal and is usually marinated to provide some tenderness. It is essential to never cook this cut beyond medium. If you only eat well-done beef, try something else. You can make the *pomme frites* in a household deep fryer or in a large pot. For the latter I suggest using a deep-fry thermometer to get the temperature right.

Steak

1 cup (250 mL) red wine
½ cup (125 mL) Worcestershire sauce
1 tsp (5 mL) chopped fresh rosemary
1 tsp (5 mL) chopped fresh thyme
1 shallot, sliced
2 cloves garlic, minced
1 tsp (5 mL) freshly ground black pepper
1 tbsp (15 mL) dry mustard
1 x 2 ½-lb (1.2-kg) flatiron steak (whole or cut into 2 pieces)

Peppercorn Cream Sauce

reserved beef marinade
3 tbsp (45 mL) canned green peppercorns
½ cup (125 mL) 35% cream
½ tsp (3 mL) salt

Crispy Pommes Frites

8 cups (2 L) peanut oil
6 large Yukon Gold potatoes
½ cup (125 mL) cornstarch
1 tsp (5 mL) sea salt or fleur de sel

For the steak:

Mix all ingredients except steak in a bowl and pour into a re-sealable freezer bag large enough to hold all the meat. Add beef to marinade in the bag and refrigerate at least 3 hours before grilling.

Light the charcoal barbecue (propane is fine too) and allow the coals to burn down to a hot ember bed. You are looking for high heat for this recipe so use lots of coals. If using propane, allow the grill to get very hot by keeping the lid of the barbecue closed for at least 10 minutes. Clean the grill well.

Drain and pat steak dry of marinade just before grilling, reserving marinade. Rub steak with 1 tablespoon of olive oil to prevent sticking to the grill. Cook for 4 to 5 minutes on each side, but to no more than medium — an internal temperature of 135°F (60°C). Rest for 15 minutes under aluminum foil before slicing into ¼-in (5-mm) slices, across the grain of the meat.

For the peppercorn sauce:

Bring marinade to a boil with all the herbs and vegetables still in it. Reduce by half and then strain sauce into a clean saucepan. Add peppercorns, cream and salt and bring to a simmer. Reduce sauce until it thickens and clings to a spoon. The sauce can be a little loose, but feel free to reduce it until it looks and tastes good to you. Keep sauce warm.

For the frites:

Preheat oil to 300°F (150°C), using a deep-fry thermometer to get the temperature right. Peel potatoes and cut into French fry batons about ¼-in (5-mm) square. Rinse under cold water and pat dry with paper towels, removing excess starch. Dust with cornstarch and shake them a bit so starch doesn't clump — you want a light coating on the fries. Fry potatoes for 3 minutes and remove, setting them on a pan lined with clean paper towels. They can be done in small batches.

Increase the oil temperature to 360°F (180°C) and refry potatoes until golden brown (crispy on the outside, soft in the middle). The second fry should take about 4 to 5 minutes if the temperature is correct. Remove from oil and sprinkle with sea salt.

Serve immediately with carved flatiron steak and warm Peppercorn Cream Sauce.

Serves 4

Desserts

Historically, in Old-World bistros, as in home kitchens in our own country, a sweet treat at the end of a meal was often made from simple items found in the larder or pantry. Cakes and puddings made from flour, eggs and sugar were most common. Wild fruits such as apples, rhubarb and berries gave variety in the right season, and preserving them in jars meant preserving the memories for later, colder months. Molasses and maple syrup gave sugary sweetness with unique flavour. Milk and cream brought crème brûlées and ice cream to the tables of restaurant goers and clotted cream into the kitchens of farmers and their families. And perhaps the week-old bread was sweetened and softened into a delicious bread pudding with raisins and brown sugar.

Today, pastry chefs have the ability to create amazing works of art with tempered chocolate and hardened sugar. And the wonder and excitement these artisans give to a meal is very special. But that is not what the desserts of a great bistro are about. The bistro chef remains concerned about letting nothing go to waste, using seasonal fruit as inspiration and taking great pride in serving a scoop of truly excellent homemade ice cream. Bistro desserts are meant to tickle our fancies with memories of childhood and warm summer nights on the back deck.

Many of the desserts featured in this chapter were contributed by the chefs not just for their "Canadian bistro" merit, but also because they are personal favourites. They prepare them at home for their families, not just in their restaurants. As you serve these dishes to your guests you can feel confident that you are dining with the very best, and that tonight's dessert will be a true Canadian bistro classic.

New Jersey Cheesecake with Rhubarb in Rosé Wine Syrup

Whether you visit a New York City deli or a bistro in Paris, Montreal or Toronto, a cheesecake is likely to be found on the menu. It is a bistro classic. The base recipe for this cheesecake comes from a business associate who hails from New Jersey, hence the name. This dessert is lighter and easier to enjoy than its New York counterpart. The cheesecake itself is one of the best I've ever tasted, but the tart rhubarb is exactly what the recipe needs to cut through the creaminess of the dessert's foundation. The rhubarb takes a bit of planning, but the beautiful rose-coloured syrup and tangy fruit will leave your guests gasping with delight.

Cheesecake Base

1 ½ cups (375 mL) graham cracker crumbs
¼ cup (60 mL) sugar
1 tsp (5 mL) cinnamon
6 tbsp (90 mL) melted butter
1 lb (450 g) cream cheese
3 eggs
1 tsp (5 mL) lemon juice
¾ cup (185 mL) sugar (second amount)
2 tsp (10 mL) pure vanilla extract

Glaze

2 cups (500 mL) sour cream
3 tbsp (45 mL) sugar
1 tsp (5 mL) pure vanilla extract

Rhubarb in Rosé Wine Syrup

2 cups (500 mL) Canadian rosé wine
1 cup (250 mL) sugar
3 tbsp (45 mL) grenadine (optional)
1 whole cinnamon stick
1 tbsp (15 mL) rosewater (optional)
1 pod star anise
1 lb (450 g) fresh rhubarb
mint leaves, for garnish

For the cheesecake base:

Preheat oven to 375°F (190°C). In a bowl, combine graham cracker crumbs, sugar, cinnamon and melted butter, and mix well. Press mixture into the bottom of a 9-in (23-cm) springform pan to a ¼-in (5-mm) thickness.

In a stand mixer fitted with a paddle attachment, beat cream cheese until smooth (about 10 minutes), scraping down the sides of the bowl and the beater once or twice during that time. Add eggs, one at a time, followed by lemon juice, sugar (second amount), and vanilla. Beat until all ingredients are incorporated and mixture is smooth.

Pour mixture onto crust and bake for 25 to 30 minutes, until set but still with a bit of movement in the centre of the filling. Let cool on the counter for at least 30 minutes.

For the glaze:

Preheat oven to 475°F (245°C). Whisk sour cream together with sugar and vanilla until smooth. Once cheesecake has cooled, pour sour cream mixture over top. Bake for 5 minutes. Let cool at room temperature for 1 hour, then refrigerate for at least 6 hours before attempting to remove cake from the springform pan.

When slicing cheesecake, dip a knife into hot water, dry it quickly on a towel, and make your slice. Repeat for every slice to ensure clean cuts and a neat presentation. Another trick is to use a length of dental floss that can cut through the entire diameter of the cake at one time, and is then pulled out through the side.

For the syrup:

Combine wine, sugar, grenadine, rosewater, cinnamon stick and star anise in a saucepan and bring to a boil. Reduce liquid by half and allow to cool completely.

Prepare rhubarb by trimming off white bottoms. Cut fruit into batons about 3 in (7.5 cm) long. Remove star anise pod and cinnamon from cold syrup and place the rhubarb in the saucepan. Bring to a boil and immediately remove from the heat, allowing fruit to steep in syrup. This will prevent rhubarb from turning mushy. If syrup looks a little thin, simply remove rhubarb and boil down again until it reaches the right consistency.

Serve about 3 batons of rhubarb on the top (or the side) of each slice of cheesecake and drizzle a tablespoon or so of the syrup over it. Garnish with a few mint leaves.

Serves 12

Maple Syrup Pie with Crème Fraîche

Charles Part, Restaurant Les Fougères, Chelsea, Quebec

Maple syrup touches on so many of our provinces' cultures and has become a signature ingredient in our culinary landscape. Chef Part calls this recipe for traditional maple syrup pie "a celebration of freshly tapped and boiled local maple syrup." Using breadcrumbs to thicken the syrup as it boils and reduces is the traditional way to make this dish and reminds him of eating maple taffy off the snow as a child. This is a treat of a dessert, a truly Canadian bistro experience. The crème fraîche is needed to cut the sweetness. An unsweetened whipped cream is a good substitute, and I have even tried it with vanilla ice cream.

Crème Fraîche
1 cup (250 mL) whipping cream
1 cup (250 mL) sour cream

Filling
3 cups (750 mL) maple syrup
3 cups (750 mL) fresh white breadcrumbs

Pastry
2 cups (500 mL) flour
1 cup (250 mL) chopped, cold, unsalted butter
¼ tsp (1 mL) salt
⅔ cup (180 mL) iced water (approximately)

For the crème fraîche:
Stir cream and sour cream together. Cover loosely and leave at room temperature overnight. The next day, stir again and refrigerate.
Yields 2 cups (500 mL)

For the filling:
In a pot, stir maple syrup and breadcrumbs together. Simmer over medium heat until bubbling and reduced to a taffy-like consistency.

For the pastry:
In food processor, pulse flour with butter and salt. Add just enough water to bring pastry together. Refrigerate for a minimum of 1 hour. Roll out dough and fit into a 12-in (30-cm) tart pan (preferably with a removable bottom). Refrigerate again for 30 minutes. Preheat oven to 350°F (180°C). Pierce bottom of tart shell evenly with a fork. Bake until golden in colour. Allow shell to cool to room temperature.

Pour syrup mixture into cooled pastry shell. Bake again at 350°F (180°C) until bubbling all over. Remove from oven and cool completely. When set, cut into neat slices and serve with Crème Fraîche.

Serves 8 to 10

Strawberry Crisp with Honey Sorrel Ice Cream

Ross and Simon Fraser, Fraser Café, Ottawa, Ontario

When in season, ripe and glowing red, strawberries are nearly a perfect food. They may be available all year long, sealed in tight-lidded plastic containers, but they taste more like pink-painted parsnips. Wild strawberries, if you are lucky enough to know where to pick them, are tiny, about the size of the top of your pinky finger. Cultivated field strawberries are much more common, and as long as you buy them when they are locally sourced and hand-picked, desserts like this one will blow your mind. Ross and Simon have paired this dish with an interesting ice cream that uses a vibrant and tangy summer herb called *sorrel*. Easy to grow and a perennial, it has a flavour somewhat like a strawberry squeezed with lemon, making it a logical accompaniment to this crisp dessert.

Honey Sorrel Ice Cream

2 cups (500 mL) 2% milk
2 cups (500 mL) 35% cream
½ fresh vanilla pod, seeds scraped
10 egg yolks
1 ¼ cups (310 mL) liquid honey
1 tbsp (15 mL) chopped sorrel

Crisp Topping

¼ cup (60 mL) sugar
½ cup (125 mL) flour
½ cup (125 mL) butter
¼ cup (60 mL) cornmeal
¼ cup (60 mL) oats

Strawberries

4 cups (1 L) fresh strawberries
¼ cup (60 mL) sugar
¼ cup (60 mL) apple juice
2 tsp (10 mL) pure vanilla extract
2 tbsp (30 mL) high-quality aged balsamic vinegar
3 tbsp (45 mL) sorrel, thinly sliced (chiffonade)

For the ice cream:

In a heavy-bottomed pot, bring milk, cream and vanilla seeds and pod to the boil. In a mixing bowl, whisk together egg yolks, honey and sorrel, then slowly add hot mixture into eggs, stirring constantly to avoid cooking yolks. Return mixture to the saucepan on very low heat, constantly stirring until it thickens. It's ready when it coats the back of a spoon. Strain the custard into a stainless steel bowl and set on ice to cool quickly, then churn in an ice cream maker, according to the manufacturer's instructions.

For the crisp topping:

Combine all ingredients in a food processor and blend until it reaches a coarse texture. Bake on a sheet pan at 325°F (165°C), until golden brown. Once cool, crumble by hand and reserve.

For the strawberries:

In a pan, combine 1 cup (250 mL) of strawberries, sugar, apple juice and vanilla and cook on low heat until reduced and concentrated, then purée in a blender until smooth. Refrigerate until ready to assemble the dessert.

Slice remaining strawberries, combine with strawberry purée and season to taste with balsamic vinegar.

Presentation:

Fill a 3-in (7.5-cm) ring mould with sliced strawberries and purée and top with crisp. Serve with a scoop of Honey Sorrel Ice Cream and garnish with a fine chiffonade of sorrel.

Serves 8

Poutines à Trou (Dumplings with a Hole) with Rum Butter Sauce and Vanilla Bean Crème Anglaise

Darren Lewis, Chives Canadian Bistro, Halifax, Nova Scotia

This dessert is well known and well loved by Acadians all over southeastern New Brunswick. These confections are essentially little apple, cranberry and/or raisin pies formed into balls, with a hole cut in the top to act as a vent during cooking and into which to pour the accompanying sauce when serving. They are mostly served still warm from the oven with a brown sugar sauce. This version is an interpretation of the old Acadian classic, served with warm rum butter sauce and a vanilla bean Crème Anglaise. It is a late-summer version that uses pear and apple combined, but it can be made with whichever orchard fruit you desire.

Crust

2 ½ cups (625 mL) flour
4 tsp (20 mL) baking powder
½ tsp (3 mL) salt
2 tbsp (30 mL) white sugar
¼ cup (60 mL) lard or unsalted butter
¾ cup (185 mL) milk
1 tbsp (15 mL) sugar, for dusting

Filling

4 cooking apples, peeled, cored and diced small
2 cooking pears, peeled, cored and diced small
½ cup (125 mL) golden raisins
½ cup (125 mL) dried cranberries
pinch of salt
2 tbsp (30 mL) brown sugar
¼ tsp (1 mL) ground cloves
1 egg, beaten (for eggwash)

Rum Butter Sauce

¾ cup (185 mL) butter
1 cup (250 mL) brown sugar
2 oz (60 mL) spiced rum

Vanilla Bean Crème Anglaise

1 vanilla bean pod
1 cup (250 mL) 10% cream
3 egg yolks
¼ cup (60 mL) sugar

For the crust:

Sift together flour, baking powder, salt and sugar. Cut lard into flour mixture until it is well coated and broken down into pea-sized pieces. Add milk and mix together to form dough. Wrap in plastic wrap and refrigerate for at least 1 hour.

For the filling:

Simply combine all ingredients except beaten egg in a bowl and mix well.

Roll out dough on a lightly floured surface to a ¼-in (5-mm) thickness. With a 5-in (13-cm) diameter round pastry cutter, cut out 12 disks. Divide filling evenly into centres of disks. Moisten edge of dough lightly with eggwash. Carefully bring edges of dough up to meet and fully close in the centre, creating a ball. Invert poutines onto a parchment-covered cookie sheet. Cut a ½-in (1 cm) round hole in top centre of each poutine, brush with a light coating of eggwash and dust entire surface with sugar. Bake for 30 to 35 minutes in a preheated 375°F (190°C) oven.

For the rum butter sauce:

Melt butter and brown sugar together over medium-high heat until sugar is dissolved. Remove from heat and carefully add rum (use caution — the rum may ignite). Return the pan to the heat and cook out until sauce has a clear, amber appearance. Keep sauce at room temperature for use in the dessert.

For the crème anglaise:

Cut vanilla pod in half lengthwise. Using the back of a paring knife, scrape out seeds and add pods and seeds to cream. Bring mixture to a simmer, remove from the heat, cover and let steep for 15 to 20 minutes. Remove pods in a separate bowl, mix egg yolks and sugar together until smooth. Temper egg mixture with warm cream (by adding warm cream to eggs in small amounts while whisking continuously). Place in a double boiler on medium heat, and stir mixture constantly until it thickens enough to coat the back of a wooden spoon. Pass sauce through a fine-meshed sieve to ensure a lump-free sauce. Chill in a bowl of iced water, then refrigerate covered. This sauce is served cold.

Presentation:

Make a pool of Crème Anglaise in the centre of a dessert plate. Place one or two poutines (depending on your appetite), warm from the oven, on top of sauce. Pour rum sauce into holes in poutines and drizzle over the top of the poutines crusts. Garnish with some whipped cream, if desired.

Serves 6 (yields 12 poutines)

Field Strawberries with Ice Wine Sabayon

Mark Gabrieau, Gabrieau's Bistro, Antigonish, Nova Scotia

Mark Gabrieau has many great attributes as a chef and restaurateur, but he has always excelled in the pastry arts. His desserts are approachable and delicious — so many other cooks make things look pretty with spun sugar and chocolate moulds but forget the flavour. Bistro desserts should be even more about simplicity than the dishes that preceded them on the menu. When working with perfectly ripe, in-season strawberries, Mark knows not to mess around with them too much. Canadian ice wine and strawberries is a common pairing, making this dessert a bistro classic. When making sabayon, serve it without delay, as it will lose some foaminess and begin to separate if it is allowed to stand.

4 large egg yolks

3 tbsp (45 mL) sugar

3 oz (90 mL) ice or late-harvest wine

½ tsp (3 mL) lemon juice

4 cups (1 L) cleaned and hulled fresh strawberries

3 tbsp (45 mL) white sugar (for brûlée tops)

In a stainless steel bowl, beat egg yolks until foamy. Beat in sugar, wine and lemon juice. Place the bowl over a pot of simmering water and continue beating until sabayon is thick and hot.

Divide strawberries into 6 bowls. Cover with sabayon, sprinkle with a small amount of sugar (about 1 tsp / 5 mL per serving) and torch the top with a propane or butane torch until lightly caramelized.

Serves 6

Okanagan Fruit Upside Down Cake with Lemon Thyme Ice Cream

Melanee Peers, Cabana Bar and Grille, Kelowna, British Columbia

Melanee Peers works as pastry chef with Ned Bell and has offered this delicious dessert cake that uses any orchard fruits in peak season. She has prepared it with apricots, pears and plums, but in this case she is using peaches that are so very popular in the Okanagan Valley. The ice cream is stunning, either with the cake or on its own. Melanee enjoys experimenting with fresh herbs in her ice cream making and the flavours of lemon, fresh thyme, peach and an earthy bit of sweet cornmeal in this dessert are wonderful.

Topping

½ cup (125 mL) melted unsalted butter

¾ cup (180 mL) dark brown sugar (or white sugar for lighter coloured fruit)

½ cup (125 mL) fruit juice (orange or a juice of the fruit chosen)

2 tsp (10 mL) vanilla extract or paste

2 cups (500 mL) ripe pitted fruit of your choice (such as peaches, apricots or cherries)

Cake Batter

¾ cup (180 mL) buttermilk

½ cup (125 mL) melted unsalted butter

4 eggs

1 tsp (5 mL) vanilla extract or paste

1 ½ cups (375 mL) all-purpose flour or pastry flour

¾ cup (180 mL) sugar

¼ cup (60 mL) cornmeal

1 tsp (5 mL) baking powder

½ tsp (3 mL) baking soda

½ tsp (3 mL) salt

Lemon Thyme Ice Cream

2 cups (500 mL) 35% cream

2 cups (500 mL) whole milk

8 stems fresh thyme, washed and dried

zest of 1 lemon

8 large egg yolks

1 cup (250 mL) granulated sugar

pinch of salt

juice of 1 lemon

For the topping:

Melt butter in a saucepan, stir in brown sugar, fruit juice and vanilla. Mix until smooth and pour into a sprayed 10-in (25-cm) cake pan. If using a springform pan, wrap the base with aluminum foil to prevent caramel from leaking out. Slice fruit and arrange on top of caramel sauce in an even layer. Set aside while you make the batter.

For the cake batter:

Combine wet ingredients (buttermilk, butter, eggs and vanilla) in one bowl. In a second bowl, sift together dry ingredients, then combine with the wet. Mix until batter is smooth. Spoon on top of fruit and gently smooth surface with a rubber spatula.

Place prepared cake onto a baking sheet and bake at 350°F (180°C) for approximately 35 minutes, or until cake is cooked in the middle (this can be tested by inserting a skewer or toothpick into the middle). Remove cake from the oven and rest for 10 minutes on a cooling rack. Flip cake upside down onto a plate. Remove the cake pan carefully as syrup and cake are both hot.

Serves 12

For the ice cream:

Prepare an ice bath, a large bowl with ice and water for cooling ice cream base.

Bring cream, milk, thyme stems and lemon zest to a simmer over medium heat. Remove from the heat and cover the pot with plastic wrap (this helps steep the flavours). In a medium-sized bowl, whisk together egg yolks, sugar and salt. Remove the plastic wrap from the pot and bring cream mixture to a simmer again. Remove about ½ cup (125 mL) of hot cream mixture and whisk it slowly into egg yolk mix, tempering eggs so they do not curdle. Add tempered egg mixture back into cream, using a spatula to remove all of it from the bowl. Clip an instant-read thermometer on the edge of the pot. Place the pot back over low heat, stirring constantly with a heat-resistant spatula. Once ice cream base reaches 170°F (77°C), dip the spatula in, bring it out and run your finger along it. The mix should hold a clean line. If it appears too thin, cook for a further minute or two.

Have another clean, dry bowl sitting in your prepared ice bath and strain hot ice cream mixture through a fine sieve into the bowl. Stir base occasionally to cool evenly. When base is cool, add reserved fresh lemon juice. Freeze ice cream, following the ice cream machine instructions. Once ice cream reaches soft serve consistency, transfer it to a freezer container. Allow to freeze about 4 hours. This will make it easier to scoop for the dessert.

Yields about 6 cups (1.5 L)

"Mini" Chocolate Truffle Cakes with Sauce Framboise and Chantilly Whipped Cream

John Taylor, Domus Café, Ottawa, Ontario

Domus has been on the must-visit list of Ottawa restaurants for years. John Taylor is a champion of promoting not only seasonal and locally sourced foods, but also the farms they come from. Any great restaurant with a good many years under its belt develops signature dishes that are requested by returning guests. This is John's signature chocolate dessert. The garnishes change with the seasons, but during the summer raspberries and chocolate are certainly a classic. This is an elegant dessert when made using the plastic PVC moulds suggested here, but it can also take on a more traditional tartlet shape if you prefer.

Truffle Cake Mousse
18 oz (500 g) dark chocolate (minimum 58% cocoa)
3 cups (750 mL) 35% cream

Ganache
9 oz (275 g) 58% dark chocolate
9 oz (275 mL) 35% cream

Sauce Framboise
1 ½ cups (375 mL) fresh or frozen raspberries
3 tbsp (45 mL) framboise liqueur
2 tbsp (30 mL) sugar
3 tbsp (45 mL) raspberry preserves or good quality store-bought jam

Chantilly Whipped Cream
2 ½ cups (375 mL) 35% cream
2 tsp (10 mL) pure vanilla extract
2 tbsp (30 mL) granulated sugar

Preparing moulds:
You can find your moulds by going to the local hardware store and purchasing 2 ¼-in (5.5-cm) black PVC unions or a length of 2 ¼-in (5.5-cm) PVC pipe and cutting it into 1 ½-in (4-cm) lengths.

Line moulds with 2 ½-in (6-cm) acetate cut into 9-in (23-cm) lengths. The acetate is springy so it will push itself against the walls of the moulds. The acetate should rise a little above the top of the black PVC plastic. If you cannot get acetate then use parchment paper and cut to the same dimensions. Have the moulds ready before you start.

For the mousse:
Chop chocolate into small pieces and place in a stainless steel bowl set over a pot of simmering water. Some high-end chocolates now come in chips or "pastilles" that do not require any chopping before use. Melt chocolate, stirring gently, until shiny and smooth. Remove chocolate from the heat and reserve.

In a separate bowl or stand mixer, whip cream into soft peaks. Quickly fold cream into melted chocolate until it is fully combined. Transfer to a piping bag and pipe mousse into each lined PVC mould to the top of the black plastic but NOT the acetate. This little gap will be filled with the ganache. Refrigerate mousse cakes until ready for the ganache.

For the ganache:
Place chopped chocolate in a bowl. Heat cream and pour over chocolate, mixing until smooth and shiny. Pour over each truffle cake, just to cover mousse tops, filling to the top of the acetate collar. Return to fridge to set.

To serve, remove cakes from moulds and remove the acetate. Place one or two on a plate and serve with Sauce Framboise, a few fresh raspberries and a spoonful of Chantilly Whipped Cream. It also goes very well with good Canadian framboise liquor.

Yields 16 mini cakes or one 8-in (20-cm) tartlet

For the sauce framboise:

Combine all ingredients in a saucepan and bring to a simmer. Press through a sieve or chinois to remove raspberry seeds, and refrigerate until ready for use.

For the whipped cream:

Simply combine all ingredients in a stand mixer and whip until stiff peaks form. The cream can either be spooned or piped on tops of chocolate ganache cakes.

Quince Tart Tatin

Michael Allemeier, Mission Hill Winery, Okanagan Valley, British Columbia

When I cooked with Michael during his Estate Wine Festival in 2004, he served this wonderful version of the French bistro dessert classic, *tart tatin*. I had little previous experience working with quince, but I instantly fell in love with this fruit, which Michael believes is underused, despite the large numbers of growers who produce it in the Okanagan. It absolutely *must* be cooked first as it is bitter, hard and practically inedible when raw. But the flavours emerge with the right touch — essences of apple, pear, lychee fruit and some floral notes make it absolutely incredible in baked desserts. Serve it simply with whipped cream or vanilla ice cream so the subtle flavours of the fruit shine through.

1 ½ cups (375 mL) sugar
3 cups (750 ml) water
1 vanilla pod, split
juice and zest of 1 lemon
5 quince (about the size of a medium apple)
1 lb (450 g) all-butter puff pastry
½ cup (125 mL) unsalted butter
1 cup (250 mL) sugar

In a pot, mix sugar and water together. Add vanilla pod and lemon zest/juice and simmer for 5 minutes. Peel and core quince and cut into quarters. Be careful, as quince is very hard and dense: a sturdy knife is needed for this task. Poach quince in the syrup for 5 to 7 minutes until al dente. Let cool in syrup, and store in syrup until needed.

Preheat oven to 425°F (220°C). Roll puff pastry into an 11-in (28-cm) round on a lightly floured surface. Brush off excess flour and chill until needed.

In a tempered 9-in (23-cm) cast iron skillet that can go into the oven, place butter and melt over medium heat. Add sugar and mix together. Turn up the heat and let sugar start to caramelize. Drain quince thoroughly from syrup. Add poached quince to caramelized syrup, mix well and cook until sugar starts to brown. Very carefully arrange quince in a circle, packing them tightly. Remove the pan from the heat. Lay pastry over quince and tuck the edges around fruit to hide it all. Bake in the oven for 20 to 25 minutes, until pastry is nicely browned and syrup is bubbling. Remove from the oven and let cool for 10 minutes. Place a plate or platter on top of the pan and very carefully flip over. Pour any excess syrup over top of tart. Serve at once, as this is best still warm.

Serves 6 to 8

Brioche Bread Pudding Stuffed Apple with Honey Vanilla Ice Cream

A few years ago my parents bought an orchard property in Nova Scotia's Annapolis Valley. One day I decided to challenge myself by cooking for them using ingredients found only in the orchard, our garden and a small nearby farmer's market. This dessert was the way we ended an eight-course meal. Instantly I knew I had stumbled upon a fun and surprisingly easy way to bake apples using fruit picked right off the tree. The presentation is striking and the flavours familiar and comforting, like an inside-out apple pie.

Apples

6 baking apples (Cortland, Northern Spy or Gravenstein)
2 egg yolks
¾ cup (185 mL) 10 to 18% cream
¼ cup (60 mL) brown sugar
1 tsp (5 mL) cinnamon
½ tsp (3 mL) cloves
2 cups (500 mL) fresh brioche, diced in 1-in (2.5-cm) cubes (day old is even better)
2 tbsp (30 mL) melted butter
¼ cup (60 mL) soft seedless raisins
¼ cup (60 mL) maple syrup
2 tbsp (30 mL) brown sugar (for topping)
apple sauce (optional), for serving
Honey Vanilla Ice Cream (recipe follows)

Honey Vanilla Ice Cream

3 cups (750 mL) 35% cream
1 cup (250 mL) whole milk
½ cup (125 mL) liquid honey
¼ cup (60 mL) sugar
2 vanilla beans, split
4 egg yolks

For the apples:

Carefully core apples while keeping them whole — an apple corer is ideal, but a paring knife can also be used. Using a channel knife or lemon zester, make a single ribbon slice from top to bottom of the apple, turning the apple as you make the cut. This will produce a spiral slice that starts at the top and ends at the bottom about ⅛ in (3 mm) deep.

In a bowl, beat together egg yolks, cream, brown sugar, cinnamon and cloves. Add brioche bread, melted butter and raisins and combine well, allowing custard to soak through the bread. Fill cavity of each apple with bread pudding mixture to the top, pressing down as you do so. Drizzle each apple with maple syrup, and sprinkle a small amount of brown sugar on bread pudding visible at the top of each apple. Bake in a 350°F (180°C) oven for 30 minutes, glazing with maple syrup every 10 minutes or so.

Rest baked apples on a small pool of simple apple sauce (optional) and top with a round scoop of Honey Vanilla Ice Cream.

Serves 6

For the ice cream:

Heat cream, milk, honey, sugar and vanilla bean pods in a heavy-bottomed saucepan, stirring occasionally until sugar is dissolved and mixture is hot. Place egg yolks in a bowl and whisk briefly. Still whisking, slowly pour in about 1 cup (250 mL) of the hot liquid. When mixture is smooth, slowly pour liquid back into the saucepan, whisking constantly. Cook over medium heat, stirring constantly, until mixture thickens slightly and coats the back of a spoon, about 8 minutes, or reaches a temperature of 170°F (77°C). Be sure not to let the mixture boil at any time or it will curdle. Remove vanilla beans, scrape out seeds and add to custard base. If using vanilla extract, add to base after straining.

Cool custard base quickly by setting the bowl in a large iced-water bath. Stir well and then refrigerate until base is very cold. Using an electric household ice cream maker, churn custard following the manufacturer's instructions. Freeze ice cream in a deep freeze for at least 4 hours before attempting to scoop it onto the dessert.

Yields 5 cups (1.25 litres)

Nova Scotia Blueberry Grunt with Buttermilk Dumplings and Fresh Cream

A wonderfully simple dessert, blueberry grunt is distinctly Nova Scotian. Families have been making this concoction of blueberries and simple soft dumplings for a very long time. I have done very little to personalize this recipe at all, though I have added a few of my favourite spices for some extra flair. Whipped cream or vanilla ice cream is a good side to this, but in the old days it would be drizzled with fresh, cool cream. It's best to make it in a casserole or stovetop dish with a lid and serve it out family style, as a tight lid is needed so the dumplings steam properly.

4 cups (1 L) fresh or frozen wild blueberries
½ cup (125 mL) sugar
½ cup (125 mL) wild blueberry juice
1 stick cinnamon
1 pod star anise
juice and zest of 1/2 lemon
2 cups (500 mL) flour
1 tbsp (15 mL) baking powder
2 tsp (10 mL) sugar
a pinch of salt
3 tbsp (45 mL) unsalted butter
⅓ cup (85 mL) buttermilk

In either a stovetop-safe casserole dish or stovetop pan with a lid, combine blueberries, sugar, blueberry juice, cinnamon stick, star anise pod and lemon and bring to a simmer.

In a mixing bowl, combine flour, baking powder, sugar and salt. Using a fork or your fingers, cut in butter. Add buttermilk and mix until a soft doughy batter forms. The batter should be slightly wetter than a typical biscuit dough, so add a bit more buttermilk if needed. Drop dough in small balls (about the size of a golf ball) on top of blueberries and 1 in (2.5 cm) apart. Place the lid on the dish and steam for exactly 15 minutes without lifting the lid. Serve in the centre of the table with a side of fresh cream.

Serves 6 to 8

Vanilla Bean Crème Brûlée

Phillippe Dupuy, Le Saint-O, Ottawa, Ontario

Phillippe is serving incredible French bistro food in a residential neighbourhood in Ottawa. "Bistro" historically implies a French restaurant, although the term has expanded to become cross-cultural. But clearly many of the bistros that dot our country remain truly French-inspired, keeping many classic dishes on their menus. There are very few chefs in Canada who have not made crème brûlée. This one was served to me for dessert at Le Saint-O one winter evening, and I think it is brilliant. It is also a nice recipe for beginners, as the custard is not cooked first. Simply combine the ingredients and bake.

8 large egg yolks
½ cup (125 mL) sugar
seeds from 2 vanilla pods
4 cups (1 L) 35% cream
2 quarts (2 L) hot water (for the bain marie)
½ cup (125 mL) white sugar (for brûlée tops)

Preheat oven to 300°F (150°C). In a bowl, mix egg yolks, sugar and vanilla bean seeds. Whisk mixture until creamy and lightened in colour. Gently whisk in cream until custard is smooth. Pour custard into 6 large crème brûlée ramekins, preferably no more than 1 ¼-in (3-cm) high. (This will allow custard to cook evenly.) Place ramekins in a roasting pan and set on the middle rack of the oven.

When brûlées are on the rack, and not before, pour hot water into the pan, about halfway up the sides of the dishes. Bake for 35 to 60 minutes, depending on your oven. Remove brûlées when custard is set but still jiggles in the very centre. Some judgment is required here. Allow brûlées to sit in the warm water for 30 minutes on the counter to finish cooking gently. Refrigerate for a minimum of 4 hours before serving.

When ready to serve, sprinkle each brûlée with an even coating of sugar, about 1 tbsp (15 mL) each. Use a propane or butane torch to melt and caramelize sugar in a sweeping motion across the top of each dish. Rest for a couple of minutes to let sugar cool, and serve.

Serves 6 or 8 (depending on size of ramekins)

Lemon Tart

Steve Vardy, Black Cat Bistro, Ottawa, Ontario

This is a simple lemon dessert that finishes any meal — spring, summer, fall, or winter — with a blast of tart pleasure. Although the greatest chefs in Canada cook locally and seasonally, certain items in the culinary world are standards that simply cannot be replaced. Can you imagine cooking without chocolate, coffee, tea, vanilla, olive oil or lemons? Would your autumn apple pie be half as good without sugar and a touch of cinnamon? Some foods have been traded globally for a long time and do not take away from the local economy. Choose organic when you can, buy fairly traded coffee, tea and chocolate, and cook with lemons. This dessert from Steve's pastry shop is a good place to start.

Dough

1 ½ cups (375 mL) all-purpose flour
½ cup plus 1 tbsp (140 mL) icing sugar
½ cup (125 mL) unsalted butter, diced
grated zest of 1 lemon
seeds from 1 vanilla pod
1 egg
flour, for dusting

Filling

5 eggs
1 cup (250 mL) sugar
zest of 2 lemons
juice of 3 lemons
½ cup (125 mL) 35% cream
¼ cup (60 mL) granulated white sugar (for brûlée tops)
icing sugar, for garnish
sprigs of mint, for garnish

For the tart dough:

Sift flour and icing sugar, and work in butter with a fork or pastry cutter. Make a well in flour mixture, and add lemon zest and vanilla grains. Beat egg and add to the well. Knead mixture with your fingers quickly but very thoroughly until smooth, then wrap in plastic film and leave to cool in the fridge for at least 30 minutes or overnight.

Preheat oven to 350°F (180°C). Cut pastry into 6 equal pieces and roll out on a lightly floured surface to a size just large enough to fill your flan tins, which should be 3 ⅜ in (8 cm) in diameter and ⅝ in (1.5 cm) in height, with a removable base (these can be found at any good quality kitchen supply store). Grease the tin, and place dough into it, gently easing it into the corners and ensuring an overhang of not less than ⅜ in (1 cm). Carefully trim overhang with a sharp paring knife. Line the flan with greaseproof paper and fill with enough dry baking beans to ensure the sides as well as the base are weighted. Bake in the oven for 10 minutes.

Remove beans and greaseproof paper, and return the flan to the oven for a further 10 minutes.

For the lemon filling:

In a large bowl, whisk eggs with sugar and lemon zest. When mixture is smooth, stir in lemon juice, then fold in cream. Continue to whisk until all ingredients are thoroughly incorporated, and remove any froth from the top.

Reduce oven temperature to 250°F (120°C). Pour cold filling into hot pastry, which ensures that the pastry case will be sealed and hold the filling. Bake for 20 to 30 minutes, depending on your oven's heat, being very careful not to overcook (the tarts will continue to cook when removed from the oven). Cool to room temperature and remove from the tart moulds.

Presentation:

Sprinkle a little sugar over each tart and brûlée with a blowtorch to caramelize the surface. Garnish with a little dusting of icing sugar and a sprig of mint.

Makes 6 small tarts (or 1 large, 10-in, 25-cm tart)